Manage It!

Hacks for Improving Your Dog's Behavior

Juliana DeWillems KPA CTP, CDBC

Wenatchee, Washington U.S.A.

Manage It!
Hacks for Improving Your Dog's Behavior
Juliana DeWillems

Dogwise Publishing
A Division of Direct Book Service, Inc.
403 South Mission Street, Wenatchee, Washington 98801
1-509-663-9115, 1-800-776-2665
www.dogwisepublishing.com / info@dogwisepublishing.com
© 2024 Juliana DeWillems

Interior: Lindsay Davisson
Cover design: Erika Austin

Library of Congress Cataloging-in-Publication Data
Names: DeWillems, Juliana, 1989- author.
Title: Manage it! : hacks for improving your dog's behavior / Juliana
   DeWillems, KPA CTP, CDBC.
Description: Wenatchee, Washington, U.S.A. : Dogwise Publishing, [2024]
|
   Includes bibliographical references and index. | Summary: "In this book,
   you will gain an understanding of what management is and how to use it,
   as well as learn about dog behavior and the science of learning.
   Ultimately, Manage It! is about supporting and enriching the
    human-canine bond through behavior-change solutions that work for
both ends of the leash"-- Provided by publisher.
Identifiers: LCCN 2024017438 | ISBN 9781617812910 (paperback)
Subjects: LCSH: Dogs--Training. | Dogs--Behavior. | Operant condition-
ing.
Classification: LCC SF431 .D495 2024 | DDC 636.7/0887--dc23/
eng/20240517
LC record available at https://lccn.loc.gov/2024017438

ISBN: 9781617812910   Printed in the U.S.A.

Table of Contents

More Praise for *Manage It!*

Finally, a book that concisely and compassionately communicates the power of small environmental changes to improve our dogs' behaviors. In it, you'll find dozens of actionable tips to create a happier home & to further any training plan. What a relief!

Kathy Sdao, MA, author of *Plenty in Life is Free: Reflections on Dogs, Training and Finding Grace*

A wonderful resource for not only dog guardians but professional dog trainers to have in their library. With detailed easy to understand descriptions Juliana shows us the hows and whys to manage any situation.

Emily Larhlam, creator of the "Dog Training by KikoPup" YouTube channel, owner of Dogmantics Dog Training

I am a huge fan of management for unwanted dog behaviors and strongly agree with author Juliana DeWillems that management isn't given enough credit in the canine behavior and training world. This book is a delightful blend of science-based and useful information presented in a well-written, easily accessible style, jam-packed with great management solutions that any dedicated dog guardian will be able to understand and implement with reasonable ease. A great addition to any dog-lover's bookshelf!

Pat Miller, CBCC-KA, CPDT-KA author of *Beware Of The Dog - Positive Solutions For Aggressive Behavior In Dogs,* owner of Peaceable Paws

Finally, a resource that provides strategies busy families can implement immediately to manage their dogs' troublesome behaviors - what a relief! As a dog and child specialist, I frequently encounter families who are struggling with dogs who steal kids' toys, chase newly mobile toddlers, or knock over visitors. This book contains insight into why the dog might be engaging in these shenanigans, along with practical hacks for how to prevent them in the future. Juliana's approachable style and clear guidance make these strategies accessible to everyone, ensuring that dogs can thrive both at home and out in the real world. This book is a must-have resource for every dog family.

Michelle Stern, CPDT-KA, Certified Canine Behavior Counselor, FDM and founder of Pooch Parenting

Manage It! is a game-changer for dog owners everywhere. Juliana DeWillems offers a refreshingly new approach to dog training that I think all dog owners can appreciate. What sets *Manage It!* apart is its accessibility and practicality. DeWillems's writing is engaging and straightforward, making complex concepts in dog training easily understandable for readers of all backgrounds. This book is for realists, for busy families, for new pet owners, for real dog owners. DeWillems highlights a fundamental truth often overlooked in the world of dog training: while training is important, management is the essential foundation for success.

From door and window issues to counter surfing, barking in the car, leash walking, and beyond, she covers a comprehensive range of topics with clarity and depth. She recognizes the needs of both dogs and their human families, offering solutions that are realistic and compassionate. By acknowledging the challenges faced by busy pet owners and cutting through the noise of contradictory information, she provides a beacon of clarity and guidance in a crowded landscape of dog training advice. I already foresee dog trainers having this book in their reference library but also in the hands of their clients. This is going to be a go to resource for many years to come.

Breanna Norris, MSc, KPA CTP, owner of Canine Insights

Manage It! reminds us that there is a time and place for the window clings, baby gates, and even tethers. Not everything needs to be a training moment - gasp! The use of QR codes throughout the book is a great addition for those of us that prefer visual learning. Manage

It! will help you both inside the home and outside on adventures with your pup. Whether you are dealing with a dog that is chewing up everything you own or barking and lunging on a walk there is something for everyone to take from this book, even us "seasoned professionals" can use the reminders this book shares.

Karen A Chapdelaine, CDBC, ADT, CPDT-KA, FFCP, DN-CET, owner of The Timeless Dog, creator of the Senior Dog Enrichment Plans: Accommodations & Adaptations webinar

Manage It! is a concise and long overdue companion to all of the wonderful training, behavior, and enrichment resources out now. Juliana provides clear and actionable strategies, methods, and recommendations for dog guardians to have immediate "wins" in regards to behavior change and success with very common training and behavior concerns. Manage It! represents a shift of culture in the training and behavior world from complicated training plans to logical applications of environmental change and understanding of normal dog behavior.

Emma R. Schneidkraut, KPA CTP, CPDT-KA, CCUI, FDM owner of A Dog's Eye View

Finally, a book about dog behavior that showcases the importance, necessity, and almost magical results of management! Manage It! provides multiple realistic solutions for common behavior problems. Anyone who needs management ideas will appreciate this book!

Allie Bender, CDBC, CPDT-KA, SBA, co-author of *Canine Enrichment for the Real World* and *Canine Enrichment for the Real World Workbook*, co-host of Enrichment for the Real World Podcast, co-owner of Pet Harmony, LLC

Management is such an important component of animal welfare and household harmony, and yet it is also one of the most underrated and misunderstood components of animal care. In this book, Juliana does a beautiful job of explaining how and why management matters, defining its role in accessible and equitable support for a wide diversity of pet parents, and articulating the relationship between management and enrichment. She then dives into the details of how to create a management plan for the most common scenarios where dog owners need support, including practical tools like worksheets and QR codes to videos and other resources. The result is a book that is a powerful tool for pet parents and pet professionals alike, and one I will be recommending to clients and students for years to come.

Emily Strong, CDBC, CPDT-KA, SBA, co-author of *Canine Enrichment for the Real World* and *Canine Enrichment for the Real World Workbook*, co-host of Enrichment for the Real World Podcast, co-owner of Pet Harmony, LLC

All dog guardians need this book! Juliana DeWillems' "Manage It!" is packed with practical, do-able advice to address common challenges pet guardians encounter. DeWillems' warm and relatable writing style makes training concepts easy to understand and apply. The book offers a wealth of useful information and even includes tools like worksheets, social media links, and videos to help guardians succeed. Highly recommend!

Veronca Sanchez, M.Ed. CDBC, CPDT-KA Founder, Cooperative Paws Service Dog Coach™, author of *Service Dog Coaching - A Guide for Pet Dog Trainers*

This is it! This is the book the training world has been missing. Not only will it help clients build better relationships with their dogs, it will also help them prevent many behavior problems from ever getting a foothold. So many pet owners believe that training is a difficult process that takes loads of time and often fails because it requires special skills beyond their reach. Juliana has the answer to all of their concerns. She has a way of making things easy to understand without oversimplifying, and that is truly a gift. I cannot recommend this book highly enough. It should be required reading for new do owners as well as those beginning a career in dog training. This book is going to be a must-read or every client I work with from now on.

Sarah Kalnajs, B.A., CDBC, CPDT-KA, AABP-CDBT, owner of Blue Dog Training and Behavior LLC

Most dog guardians want to live a happy, fulfilled life with their canine companions. However, behavior concerns tend to cause a strain in the relationship. Juliana does a wonderful job providing the reader with practical advice and educational videos to prevent and address common behavior concerns. Every dog guardian should have a copy!

Marissa Martino, CDBC host of the Paws & Reward Podcast. author of *Human-Canine Behavior Connection. Building Better Relationships Through Dog Training*

In a world of quick fixes and "life hacks," training our dogs can feel overwhelming, especially when dealing with multiple problem behaviours and situations. Using management is as close to a "life hack" as we will get in training, and Juliana's book is a must-read for anyone dealing with these issues. This makes training easier, makes your life easier, and allows your dog to "get it right." It can seem too easy, but just as we baby-proof our houses, management can be an excellent addition to training or, in some cases, can replace training altogether!

Emily Priestley, CTC, CDBC, podcast host of The Wild at Heart Podcast, author of *Urban Sheepdog*

An entire book on management? Sign me up! Juliana is a master at presenting simple yet incredibly helpful information to the typical pet parent. Management is an often overlooked step in training. Not anymore! This book provides all the information you need to manage your dog's behavior effectively.

Cassie Pestana, CBCC-KA, KPA-CTP, founder of Clickstart Dog Training Academy, LLC, graduate of Brown University with a Bachelor of Arts in Biology (Ethology & Evolutionary Biology)

I recommend this unique book to everyone who touches a dog's life. Juliana DeWillems understands and appreciates the strong bond between our dogs and ourselves and the cultural strains which often crop up between the canine and human worlds. Take your first step to change how you look at the way your dog perceives the world and how you work with behavioral missteps your dog makes. As Juliana says: "(managing the dog's environment) …empowers people to make positive changes." Buy this book!

Manage It! is an essential read for anyone who interacts with dogs – trainer, pet parent, dog sport coach, shelter worker, service dog guardian, veterinarian and more. Juliana's empathy towards both humans and dogs shines through her words as she encourages us all to take steps towards managing what we may not have the time to train. Experience powerful, positive ways to improve your relationship with your dog by picking up this book. You won't regret it.

Linda Randall, DVM, KPA CTP, Tagteach Level 3, owner of One Smart Dog

Introduction

Most of us see dogs as part of our family and love nearly everything about them. However, there are always going to be behaviors from our dogs that we might want to change. This book outlines simple, effective ways to change your dog's behavior that do not fall under conventional training recommendations. Known as management, these solutions focus on preventing unwanted behaviors from occurring, leading to a more harmonious life with your dog. Each chapter dives into a different behavior issue that dog guardians commonly face. At the end of the book you will find a recommended reading list, resources you can access online, and a management hack worksheet you can use to track your progress.

As a Certified Dog Behavior Consultant, management is a critical part of my work with clients. Management is what can give a family immediate relief from the challenging behavior they are experiencing from their dog and allow for progress to be built from there. Sometimes management prevents my dog training services from being needed at all. While some dog training books touch on the concept of management, there is no other book in print that is focused as much on using this powerful technique as this book. I believe that there is an enormous need for the general public to learn more about this life-changing approach to dog behavior.

In this book, you will gain an understanding of what management is and how to use it, as well as learn about dog behavior and the science of learning. Ultimately, *Manage It!* is about supporting and enriching the human-canine bond through behavior-change solutions that work for both ends of the leash.

Throughout this book you will see QR codes that link to applicable resources. If you hold your phone camera up to the QR code, the URL will pop up and you can click on the link.

If for some reason the QR codes don't work, you can find all the videos on my YouTube channel: www.youtube.com/@jwdogtraining

Open the camera on your mobile device.

Focus your camera on the QR code to scan.

Tap the link that appears to access applicable resources, including videos and worksheets.

Part 1
The What and The Why

Chapter 1
What is Management?

As a dog trainer and behavior consultant, I often say to new clients: "I'm a dog trainer, not a magician. I don't have a magic wand to solve this problem!" This sentiment aims to set realistic expectations for dog guardians embarking down the road of training. We as dog trainers want you to know that lasting change takes time and requires commitment: there is no such thing as a quick fix. But what if I told you there actually is such a thing as a quick fix or "hack," and it's what this book is all about!

This book dives into a concept that in the dog training world we call **management**. Simply put, management focuses on preventing unwanted behaviors from occurring by altering parts of the environment that prompt a dog to behave in a way that you as the owner/guardian find unpleasant, such as barking at the mail carrier every time they approach your house. This means you are using the environment to increase the likelihood of the behavior you want (no barking) and, more importantly, to decrease the likelihood of the behaviors you don't (barking). The dog training industry doesn't have an exact agreed upon definition for management. It's not a scientific term, but it is rooted in the science of behavior—more on that later. For now, think of management as using your dog's environment to your advantage when trying to change their behavior.

Not only is there a lack of agreement among dog trainers on the role of management, it is not exactly a concept used and understood by most of the general public, and that lack of understanding can cause confusion. Most people think of the term "management" as something that happens in the business world. While there are a wide variety of opinions as to what makes a good business manager, they almost all agree it is the ability to influence other people to do what is best for the entire team. Sounds like dog training to me!

I once gave an entire two-hour webinar on the subject of management and when someone joined thirty minutes late, having missed the introduction, they wanted to know when I was going to get to the actual training information. I get it, if you don't have background or additional context, solutions that focus on management instead of training can seem confusing or maybe even pointless, but management is not pointless—in fact, it can be life changing. This is why I am here writing an entire book about it.

In this book you'll find two main parts: the first being background about what management is and how it ties into training and what dogs learn, and the second part being separate chapters focused on specific behavior challenges. Both parts carry equal importance when it comes to understanding how to change your dog's behavior. Let's dive in.

An ounce of prevention is worth a pound of cure

Management is meant to create a life where you immediately see less unwanted behavior from your dog. By rearranging your dog's environment, you remove the cycle where the unwanted behavior occurs and you have to repeatedly jump in to stop your dog. With proper management in place, the unwanted behavior doesn't even happen in the first place.

You might be thinking, "Well, if it really is as simple as preventing the unwanted behavior, I would have done that already!" Management doesn't occur as a solution to a lot of dog guardians because they don't see dog behavior the same way that we do as professionals. Therefore, they don't recognize opportunities to prevent unwanted behavior. So, many people immediately turn to what makes the most sense to them, which is to try to change the behavior after it has occurred. The dog jumps up on the counter to search for food, the owner yells at the dog to get down, but the dog has already snatched a tasty morsel and their behavior of "counter surfing" will likely be repeated in the future.

Some people feel apprehensive that management is not as good as "proper training" and that it is like a band-aid. This worry is usually the result of society's arbitrary and unrealistic standards when it comes to raising and training our dogs, so kudos to you for being here to learn an alternative perspective.

Some real-life scenarios

To help you fully understand what management is, let's talk about some real-life scenarios. Don't worry, I'll deep dive into these behaviors in future chapters. For now, I want to make sure we are on the same page about what management is. Remember, management focuses on changing the environment, not the dog directly. Putting a lid on your trash can to prevent your dog from getting into the garbage is an example of management. Another would be putting your shoes in the closet if your dog keeps chewing on them, or putting your dog on a leash when guests come over so he doesn't jump up on them. You might have noticed that with each of these examples you are not actually teaching your dog not to go into the trash, or chew on your shoes, or jump on guests—you are simply preventing it.

The reason you want to prevent the unwanted behavior from occurring is that every time your dog engages in the unwanted behavior, they are getting better at it, and training progress is being slowed or set back. This is true for even the most in-depth training plans that are focused on directly addressing the behavior and its root cause. No matter how much training you want to do, it will be very hard to change your dog's behavior without also doing management.

Unfortunately, by the time most people get around to implementing management to undo undesirable habits their dogs have gotten really good at. The other, and actually best-case scenario, is to proactively use management to prevent unwanted habits from forming in the first place, leaving room for shaping desirable behaviors instead. An ounce of prevention is worth a pound of cure.

Chapter 2
Management and How Dogs Learn

I need to confess something to you: while I say that management is easier than training, management actually *is* training. Dogs are always learning, and management influences what a dog will learn. Behavior science—specifically the science of learning, known as behavior analysis—informs the best practices in the dog training industry. We know a great deal about how behavior works; therefore, we know a great deal about how to change it. What we understand about how behavior interacts with the environment is called **operant conditioning**. The laws of learning are occurring whether you are aware of them or not, just like the laws of gravity. The laws of learning support the use of management, so it's important that you understand the basics. Once we get through this chapter, we'll dive back into all the ways management will be beneficial for you.

The ABCs

Behavior, what a dog does, is influenced by antecedents and consequences. **Antecedents** are the events, actions, or circumstances that happen before a behavior, and **consequences** are what happens during or after the behavior. What happens in the environment before, during, and after the behavior are known collectively as the **conditions** under which behavior occurs.

Antecedent → Behavior → Consequence

Most qualified dog behavior professionals agree that the best training practices include arranging antecedents to prevent the rehearsal of unwanted behavior—what dog trainers call management—while using positive reinforcement to teach acceptable replacement behaviors. This book will help you to recognize all the ways you can arrange antecedents to quickly and easily live a more harmonious life with your dog.

Two important things to know: behavior does not occur in a vacuum, and behavior always occurs for a reason. What this means is that something in the environment (an **antecedent**, or set of antecedents) cues your dog's behavior. Think of when a dog barks at the mail carrier. The conditions of the blinds being open allow the dog to see outside. The mail carrier walking to the house is the antecedent that cues the barking behavior. There is also a consequence to that behavior that will cause it to occur more or less frequently.

Every time your dog engages in what you consider to be an undesirable behavior, that behavior brings with it a consequence. When the consequence increases the behavior over time, we say their behavior has been **reinforced. Positive reinforcement** means that when something is added to the environment following a behavior, it increases the likelihood that the behavior will occur again in the future. Positive reinforcement is often associated with giving a dog treats during a training session, but toys, playtime, and praise can also be reinforcement options *if your dog enjoys them* and they increase the behavior over time. In addition, the environment can be rich with reinforcers for your dog, including opportunities to engage in chewing, sniffing, and destroying. Often when nuisance behaviors are occurring frequently, a **negative reinforcement** contingency can be at play. Negative reinforcement means that the consequence of removing something from the environment increases the likelihood that the behavior will happen again in the future. For example, when the mail carrier approaches your house and your dog barks, the mail carrier leaves. To the dog, the consequence of barking may have been the removal of a stranger approaching the house. The dog doesn't know that the mail carrier was planning on walking away anyway!

If a behavior is occurring, especially if it is occurring consistently, it is being reinforced in some way—even if you can't identify the reinforcer. Behaviors that get reinforced get repeated. When you use management to prevent the rehearsal of the unwanted behavior, you are also *preventing the reinforcement* that was keeping that behavior strong.

Let's use an example: Your dog jumps up and puts their front paws on the counter. Many trainers call this "counter surfing." There are a few outcomes that typically occur. One option is that you run over to your dog, put your hands on them, and guide them off the counter, maybe saying "bad dog!" while you do it. For some dogs, this attention and physical interaction could actually be something they enjoy! Something they want more of! They learn that jumping on the counter gets your attention. In this case, your effort to stop the behavior may have accidentally strengthened, or reinforced it.

Another outcome of the counter surfing behavior would be that your dog jumps on the counter and grabs the sandwich you're making. This could happen 1 out of 100 times they jump up, but that one single delicious win could reinforce their counter surfing enough that the behavior continues. Given that we are humans with imperfect behavior ourselves, this outcome is more likely than we think. Despite our best efforts, we will inevitably leave something out on the counter. Your dog learns: "A-ha! I just need to try harder, or more often, and I will score something else tasty one day!" This, as you can imagine, is reinforcing.

One other possible outcome is that your dog simply gets to scavenge and sniff while their front paws are on the counter. Scavenging is an innate need that dogs have. The act of sniffing and scavenging is going to be enjoyable for most dogs, so even if they don't actually get any food when they counter surf, the opportunity to scavenge could still reinforce their counter surfing behavior.

Additionally, many people's initial reaction is to yell at the dog, interrupt the behavior, and attempt to teach them that what they are doing is "bad" or "wrong." In other cases, people might set up a bunch of metal trays so that when the dog jumps up all the pans fall down, and the dog is so scared that they don't try it again. Others reach for more intense interventions, like correcting the dog by yanking on their collar, or spraying them with water. These are all intended to be aversive consequences following the behavior that decrease the chances the counter surfing occurs again in the future. An **aversive** is something that causes your dog to behave in a manner to escape, avoid, or prevent. **Punishment** relies on aversive consequences. Some might not think of these outcomes as punishment due to society's constructs around the topic, however the scientific definition of punishment is any consequence that decreases the likelihood of a behavior happening in the future.

If the consequence...	Then it is...
Increases the behavior over time	Reinforcement
Decreases the behavior over time	Punishment

People often think punishment will be the easiest way to fix the problem. To reinforce an alternative behavior, you have to be there and paying attention to the dog. You might be thinking, why do you want me to restrict my dog's access to the windows when I could just use a citronella bark collar to stop my dog from barking at people on the sidewalk? You might even be thinking about how a citronella collar doesn't actually *hurt* the dog, it just startles them—it interrupts and often stops the behavior, which is what you want after all! What most people don't realize is that interventions that use an aversive are *not* always harmless. The impact can go far beyond the simple interruption that most people see when they utilize bark collars, verbal corrections, spray bottles, cans filled with pennies, leash pops, etc. In fact, when our focus is only on reducing the unwanted behavior, most people don't realize just how mentally and physically harmful such techniques can be to our dogs.

It doesn't matter if someone uses one of the fluffy euphemisms that society loves: discipline, correction, feedback, clarity, etc.—the use of aversive stimuli comes with well-documented risks (see the Resources list at the end of the book for sources). The unintentional side effects are often referred to as **fallout**.

Fallout can look like:

- increased stress (observed through the dog's body language and behavior)
- avoidance of the circumstances surrounding the interaction (including avoiding you)
- increased reactivity
- increased aggression
- learned helplessness
- suppression of normal behavior, creating a "shut down" dog
- the breakdown of your relationship with your dog

Researchers are still determining what may make fallout from punishment more or less likely, and the average pet guardian cannot predict when side effects may occur. What frequently happens is that people don't know what to look for, and therefore don't realize fallout has resulted from their use of punishment. This can be especially tricky because fallout often does not occur right away—it happens over time.

Let's revisit the counter surfing example and see what happens if any time your dog jumps on the counter you pick up a spray bottle and squirt your dog with water. The first time it happens, the dog winces, tucks their tail, and runs out of the kitchen to their bed in the next room. Success, you think! They won't try that again! And they probably won't, at least not for a bit. However, the same alarm and fear that caused them to run away from the counter could also become associated with you. You're the scary one who caused the scary thing to happen. Yes, dogs can make associations like this, and unfortunately, they can occur whether we want them to or not. We have very little control over what associations are being made and when.

In this example, your dog might recover from the unsettling incident, or they could begin to avoid you when you're in the kitchen. They could also start to avoid the kitchen altogether, whether you're in it or not. They don't necessarily understand that their behavior of putting paws on the counter is what caused the water-spraying. What they do know is that the scary thing happened in the kitchen, and it came from you. They could also start to avoid you more in general, not just in the kitchen. Other side effects could include your dog running away when you pick up a bottle of cleaner to spray and wipe down the furniture, or they start to growl or lunge at you when you pick up a spray bottle.

It's important to me, as I believe it is to many guardians, to build a relationship with my dog rooted in trust. If you're realizing now that you've used punishment in the past and you're worried about how it might have impacted your relationship with your dog, fear not—now that you know differently, you can change the way you interact with your dog and approach their behavior. This book, as well as all the books in the Recommended Reading section, will help you repair or strengthen your relationship with your dog.

Some people might not mind if their dog chooses to avoid them in the name of "teaching" and "discipline." It's something I mind, and it's something I intentionally try to prevent. If you would also like to avoid the potential fallout of punishment, you're in the right place. I aim to change behavior in non-confrontational ways that don't involve fear, stress, coercion, or discomfort. Utilizing management fits exactly in line with this non-confrontational approach.

There are also practical reasons to avoid relying on punishment-based interventions. Dogs are not moral creatures—they do not understand or know right from wrong. If you're thinking right now about a moment when your dog seemed "guilty" in response to doing something "wrong," that was likely them showing appeasement behaviors to diffuse conflict. When humans are angry, our body language reads like a neon sign, and dogs can perceive our loud voice, stiff posture, furrowed brow, and direct eye contact as threatening. In response, they often offer appeasing body language like averting their gaze, putting their ears back, and putting their head down. We as humans have a tendency to anthropomorphize, attributing moral emotion to this behavior, when in reality, our dogs are simply responding to our body language, not admitting guilt.

However, dogs do learn from consequences what is and isn't "safe." Meaning, they learn under which conditions they are safe to perform a behavior without the aversive consequence occurring, and in which conditions they should avoid doing the behavior because the aversive consequence is likely to occur. We learn it is safe to speed when we don't see cop cars present because the consequence of a ticket is less likely. With the counter surfing example, dogs often learn it is safe to counter surf when the humans aren't present because it's the humans who administer the consequences. So, when relying on punishment, you might reduce the occurrence of the behavior while you are present (along with possibly creating a slew of other side effects as we discussed), but you haven't actually taught the dog to not counter surf at all times. Relying on punishment to address counter surfing may actually make you *more* likely to lose that sandwich you're making when you walk out of the room to take a phone call than if you relied on management, such as a gate, to keep your dog out of the kitchen all together.

If you've made the connection that both punishment and management aim to decrease unwanted behaviors, you're right. However, an important distinction is that punishment relies on consequences after the behavior occurs, and management prevents the behavior from occurring in the first place.

Management is not only a low-stress way of changing behavior, but it can be more effective and faster than the quick fixes often promised by punishment solutions. Management both immediately changes what behavior is more or less likely to occur in a given situation and directly impacts what your dog is rehearsing and therefore learning.

Chapter 3
Management and the
Human-Canine Bond

It is my belief that using management techniques can enhance the human-canine bond. Witnessing the bond between people and their dogs will never get old to me, will never stop filling my cup. We share our lives with these incredible four-legged beings and they become part of our family. We buy them comfy beds, we bring them on vacation, we stock up on their favorite toys, we confide in them, and we always wish we had more time with them once they're gone. There is simply no love like the love we have for our dogs.

From my experience as a trainer, the majority of people who share their lives with dogs don't actually mind a lot of canine behaviors that society might label as problematic. Overall, many of us don't mind when our dogs bark to communicate, chase squirrels, or jump up on us to say "hi." Most people love their dogs so much that a lot of normal dog behavior doesn't bother them, at least not most of the time. For the stuff here or there that might frustrate or annoy you about your dog, I have your magical and relatively easy solution: management. I feel strongly that management can strengthen the human-canine bond and make life with a dog more harmonious, which is one of the main reasons I want more people to utilize it.

When someone learns I am a dog trainer, one of the most common responses I hear is: "Oh, my dog could use some training!" I find that people sometimes feel guilt or shame over not training their dog more, or their dog not behaving like the dogs we see in movies. There is a disconnect between how the media portrays our four-legged companions and what life with them is really like. Society puts some unnecessary, unfair, and often arbitrary expectations on dogs, and on us as their guardians. Dogs are supposed to fit seamlessly into our human world and we, as their guardians, are supposed to train them to rigid perfection. I reject this whole sentiment. Dogs are dogs, and we ask too much of them when expecting adherence to the demands of the human world. We want them to walk at certain times, in certain places, in certain ways. We want them to chew on certain things, but not others. We want them to eat certain foods at certain times. In so many ways, the modern world has taken *being a dog* away from dogs.

Dogs feel frustrated because they can't behave like dogs, often causing them to manifest "nuisance" behaviors, which then frustrates us as humans. I want to point out before we move on that your dog's behavior is morally neutral. Your dog's behavior is not good or bad, it is simply behavior. This is why I specifically use terms like desirable and undesirable, or wanted and unwanted. Guardians often forget that dogs are not moral creatures, and the baggage we put on them surrounding "good" and "bad" behavior complicates our relationship and makes life together harder than it needs to be.

Expectations

Speaking of morally neutral behavior, let's talk about expectations and what is realistic in terms of your expectations of your dog. If you are hoping this book about non-training management solutions is going to turn your dog into a calm, quiet, stuffed animal like dog, this is where I have to squash that. There is so much freedom that can come with appropriately adjusting your expectations and understanding that your dog is a dog who will be a dog. Learning to see the joy in their dog-ness is much easier than constantly being frustrated by their natural, normal behavior. I say this with the desire to make living with your dog more peaceful because I empathize with the strain that can come with accommodating another living creature. Managing expectations and understanding your dog's behavior can be life changing—right up there with management!

Another way to understand your dog better is to learn what they are communicating with their behavior. Detailed analyses of dog body language and of dog behavior are, unfortunately, beyond the scope of this book, so I highly recommend reading books that are devoted to these topics so you can learn to understand what your dog is saying to you. I list some of my favorite body language resources in the Recommended Reading section at the end of this book. Dogs are always talking to us, we often just don't know how to listen. Management is only one piece of the puzzle to achieving more harmonious living between you and your dog. Understanding your dog's body language and behavior is another important piece as well.

Chapter 4
Not All Trainers You Meet
Will Agree With Me

As with most topics in the dog world, if you ask 50 different dog trainers their opinions about management, you'd likely get 50 different answers. Trainers rely on and recommend management to varying degrees. Some trainers believe that any management at all is a cop out and is irresponsible, and that all behaviors should be addressed with conventional training that focuses on teaching and changing behaviors through consequences—that guardians should get their act together and train their dogs more! I hope you have gathered by now that I am not that kind of trainer.

It doesn't bother me that other people feel differently, because I love management. I am writing a book on it after all! I think management gives you high results with low effort. I also am not one of those trainers who has very strong opinions about how much training people do or don't do with their dogs. Some trainers see dogs that society labels as "unruly" and roll their eyes, muttering about how the owner should be doing more training. I disagree. I think whatever you want your standards to be with your dog is completely fine, as long as your and your dog's quality of life is good and your dog is not a safety concern within the community, which is why management is an excellent option for most people. You may not be interested in or able to train your dog for hours and hours to change their behavior, but sure, you're willing to make some small changes to your home environment or your dog's routine. Training is often a longer process, where management can be a one and done; set it and forget it. A lot of times management can be easier and more doable for most dog guardians.

That's not to say I don't love and value training too. I am a dog trainer after all—and a skilled one at that. I recognize that plenty of people are interested in putting the time in to train their dogs, and I am happy to help those folks. My training business sees hundreds of families per year to address challenges with their dogs through training. I think training with positive reinforcement comes with so many benefits, from teaching your dog to cope with the human world, to building your bond together. Implementing positive reinforcement training can be an important part of an animal's welfare. If you want to work on training your dog around the issues you're having, I wholeheartedly support that, and there are some incredible books out there about training. My hope is that this book about management is an excellent addition to your resource library because of how management can accelerate the training process.

I also want to point out that professional training can be inaccessible to a lot of people, both financially and physically. I would be remiss if I did not point out the privilege that comes with being able to afford a dog trainer for private lessons to address specific behavior challenges. In addition, people with disabilities might not be able to fully implement some traditional training practices. This is another reason why educating dog guardians about management is so important. Management can be a more accessible option to changing behavior than training.

I recently saw another dog trainer online say that management can't actually change behavior, that you'll just have to manage forever. I disagree with this as a blanket statement. From a training perspective, when you use management and prevent the rehearsal of unwanted behavior, you are creating space and reinforcement opportunities for more desirable behaviors to occur and positive habits to be formed. Most of the time this requires some proactive training, though sometimes naturally-occurring reinforcers take over and strengthen the new replacement behavior without you even putting in much work. One example of this could be door greetings. Let's say you manage by using a gate to keep your dog—who is an enthusiastic greeter—in the living room and away from the door when people come in. This environmental change puts your dog in the perfect position to hop up on the couch in the living room to say hi to the incoming guests, instead of jumping on them at the door. Your guests say hi to your dog at the couch, which is easier for everyone because your dog jumps less, and your dog is thrilled about all the attention from the guests. This management is easy to implement, so you keep it in place for the foreseeable future. Then one day a year later you forget to put the gate up, but your dog still runs to the couch and waits for the guests to come say hi to them. The behavior of greeting people on the couch has been so heavily reinforced by the attention from the guests, while the behavior of rushing the door has had zero reinforcement, so the new habit is maintained even when the management isn't in place. The success of a behavior change like this even after you fade out the management relies on many factors, some of which are explained in later chapters, but it is very possible.

As previously mentioned, sometimes when someone learns about management they believe it's just putting a band-aid on the problem instead of actually addressing the issue. While it's true that we are not addressing the root of the issue, we are still solving a problem. We change the behavior by changing the environment, not by addressing the behavior directly. To which I say: so? Is that so bad? If you can prevent your dog from getting into the trash by buying a trash can with a lid on it and that works for you, does it matter if your dog hasn't "learned to not get into the trash"? You get to decide what works for YOU. Don't let society's definition of a "well trained" dog, or, as Dr. Susan Friedman says, "the cultural fog" of what dogs should or shouldn't do influence your family's decisions.

When I first started training dogs a decade ago, I worked with a family who had just adopted a young dog from a shelter and hired me to help them. The dog was rambunctious and full of life. Admittedly, I really didn't know what I was doing beyond teaching a few behaviors. The dog guardians complained that their dog was running into the bathrooms and stealing the toothbrushes off the sink (I chuckle thinking about this now, what a funny pup!). We spent a whole lesson trying to teach "leave it" around the toothbrushes, which, surprise, was not successful. The dog's 24/7 access to the toothbrushes made it impossible to prevent the stealing behavior 100% of the time, so inevitably she got to the toothbrushes many more times, joyfully prancing around the house while her humans chased her and tried to salvage their toothbrushes (likely a very reinforcing consequence!). Trying to rely on training alone in this instance was futile. If a client came to me with a similar concern now, I would give them two options: close the bathroom doors or find a place for the toothbrushes that the dog can't reach. Simple as that. A small change would have made a huge difference in the behavior, without much headache for anyone.

The thing is, you can, of course, change behavior through training. You can change the same behaviors through training that you can change using management but, in many cases, it is going to take you much longer. Changing behavior through training alone, without any use of management, takes hours of carefully teaching the behavior, and then taking all the necessary steps to strengthen the behavior in order to make it reliable under the conditions you want it. What most people don't realize is that the training required to create a reliable behavior—one that holds up against the everyday distractions that come with the hubbub of a household—takes a lot of work. It's not impossible, just tedious and time-consuming.

For the average person, the training requirements to change challenging behaviors long-term are often too much. Many people dream of having a dog lie calmly on a mat when guests come through the door as a replacement for the chaotic greetings that are usually a family's experience. Sure, you could train that new replacement behavior. You would need to first teach the "go to your mat" behavior, then build duration, work on distractions, and finally build up to the distraction of humans coming through the door. Each step of the training would need to be broken down into small pieces that are practiced hundreds of times. Most people start the process and teach the "go to mat" behavior, which goes well, but then they don't realize how much practice is required for the behavior to hold up. The behavior falls apart when guests come over and dog guardians end up upset. "The training didn't work!" they might say. But it did work, it worked exactly how it was supposed to—you just didn't complete the process and work through all the steps you needed to. I say this without judgment. I am simply the behavior science messenger. I cannot magically make it so that we can skip steps in the training process because the training is too tedious. We're talking about another living being learning an entirely new skill under extremely challenging conditions. To wrap your head around it, think about if you were to learn the piano and then be asked to give a full concert in front of your favorite singer. It would take so much practice and rehearsal! It's just not easy.

This is why I love management—it is easy. It fits into the busy, go-go-go world that humans function in now; a world that is often incompatible with most tedious, time-consuming training procedures. Management gets the job done and makes everyone's life easier. If you want to do training on top of management, great! If you want to use only management, great!

All this to say: there are many opinions out there about management. If you implement the strategies I lay out in this book, you might get comments from family and friends about how you're just putting a band-aid on "the real problem." My goal is for you to read the information I present here and feel comfortable in your decisions. I want to empower you to do what is best for your dog and your family, while also removing any guilt you might feel about not doing more training. Management is good enough, if it's good enough for you.

Chapter 5
Management Can Solve A Lot...But Not This

Management can be highly effective and can solve a lot of your problems, but there is one main area it cannot fix. Management cannot replace meeting your dog's needs. Dogs have innate biological needs such as sniffing, chewing, destroying, licking, digging, chasing, and exploring. All dogs have at least some of these needs. A lack of opportunities to perform species-specific behaviors can cause a lot of problems in dogs. Think about the dog who lives in an apartment and who gets two 10-minute walks a day and is otherwise expected to sleep on the couch. I would not be surprised at all if that dog was out of control on leash, chewing up their guardian's belongings, and constantly jumping on the counters. That dog has very little opportunity to *be a dog*—to stretch their legs and sniff and shred stuff!

It doesn't even have to be as extreme as the exercise-deprived apartment dog. Even dogs who do go on plenty of walks or have a large yard can still not be getting their needs met, because biological canine needs go beyond walking in a straight line on a six-foot leash or chasing a ball in a yard. There is a chance that no amount of management could curb the behaviors you're seeing from your dog if their needs are not being met—and it shouldn't. That is one area where I do *not* want a band-aid: trying to cover up issues that have emerged because a dog is unfulfilled or lacking in their opportunities to be a dog. That is not fair to the dog, and this situation is likely to produce frustration for you as well.

The good news is that those opportunities for species-specific behaviors, called **enrichment**, are relatively easy to implement. To supplement your knowledge on this topic, I highly recommend the book *Canine Enrichment for Real World* by Allie Bender and Emily Strong for a more in-depth look into enrichment and how it can change your dog's life. If you want a shorter read and you want to start ensuring your dog's needs are met, check out their companion workbook *Canine Enrichment for the Real World Workbook*. Both books are available at Dogwise.com.

Enrichment is also an area where it's actually relatively safe to turn to the internet (versus other dog training topics where misinformation on the internet runs rampant). The hashtags #Enrichment and #DogEnrichment on social media have endless examples and information about enrichment, as does good old Google. Enrichment could be anything from a food puzzle to encourage sniffing and thinking, to providing your dog with cardboard boxes to let them shred and destroy. Putting a sandbox in your backyard so your dog can dig as much as they want or letting your dog run off leash in a safe area are also good enrichment options. Basically think: how can I let my dog do doggy things in a safe way that works for both of us?

A Kong stuffed with something tasty provides your dog with an outlet for licking.

Similarly to the Kong, a Lick Mat gives your dog an opportunity to lick off whatever you smear onto the mat. Licking can be very calming for dogs.

Hiding kibble or treats in a snuffle mat provides your dog an opportunity to put their fantastic sense of smell to use.

Food puzzles are an easy way to incorporate sniffing and problem solving into meal times.

I cannot stress enough that, a lot of the time, the behavior issues my clients come to me with are improved dramatically when we focus on meeting their dog's needs. Like reading canine body language, humans don't come with an inherent understanding of what dogs need in order to feel biologically fulfilled. You can have dogs for decades and still not know that, for example, letting a dog sniff on walks is critical for their mental health. You don't know what you don't know. As a dog training professional, I can usually spot holes where the dog's needs are not being met after evaluating a dog's behavior and learning about their daily routine. The thing is, an unmet need does not always have an obvious direct impact on the behavior. For example, a dog who doesn't do much at home could be highly reactive to other dogs on walks. He is pent up, frustrated, and also experiencing anxiety. This is a bit simplified, but making sure that he has plenty of outlets to be a dog and to sniff, shred, chew, lick, etc. (which of those would depend on what he enjoys and what has an impact on his behavior) has the ability to dramatically decrease stress levels and "fill his cup" so to speak, helping him better cope with triggers on walks. When I tell a guardian of a reactive dog that we are actually not going to start with training, but instead going to implement a daily enrichment plan, I am often met with skepticism. I get it; how could this possibly help? The proof is in the behavior change over time.

So, while I love management and know that it can accomplish a lot, I want you to still be very aware of your dog's needs and how you can meet those needs. Learning how to build enrichment into your dog's daily routine (like you do with their meals, potty time, walks, etc.) will make it a sustainable habit long term. There are also a lot of do-it-yourself enrichment options so you are not adding extra expenses. Please do pursue more information about enrichment in books or online—this chapter really only barely scratches the surface.

Part 2
The How

Introduction to behavior-specific management interventions

Here we are. You've made it to the part where I tell you about actual management strategies that you can apply depending on what behavior you're dealing with. I'll be focusing on the most common behavior challenges that I hear from everyday dog guardians, which include:

- Barking at home, in the yard, on the deck, and in the car
- Jumping on guests when they arrive
- Chewing on or destroying household items
- Stealing food off the counter (also sometimes known as counter surfing)
- Barking and lunging at other dogs or people while on a walk
- Not coming when called
- Pulling on leash
- Puppy nipping
- Housetraining issues for dogs of all ages
- Inability to settle at dog-friendly patios
- Challenging vet visits
- Scratching at doors
- Getting into the trash
- Dashing out doors

By now you have the background about why we choose these interventions instead of or in addition to training, so I want to take a minute here to remind you that these are general options. Every dog and every situation is different, therefore what I recommend might not work for you, or you might need to tweak it. When I work 1-on-1 with a client I bring a concept and then adapt it to their individual situation. Unfortunately, I cannot do that through a book, but my hope is that I can give you plenty of ideas to think about, many you may not have heard of or considered before. After reading the recommendations you will have a baseline of knowledge and ideas to then adapt to your specific circumstances. If you implement anything in this book and like the outcome, please share on social media with the hashtag #ManageItBook or tag me at @jwdogtraining. This social-media-loving millennial would love to see it!

Follow me on

𝓘𝓷𝓼𝓽𝓪𝓰𝓻𝓪𝓶

SCAN ME

@jwdogtraining

Scan this to follow me on Instagram where I post training and behavior tips that are a great supplement to what you're learning in this book.

Chapter 6
Greeting Guests at the Door

A dog's behavior at the door can cause frustration and highlight the challenges of living with a dog. Many dog guardians describe their dogs as exuberant and over-the-top when someone comes to the door and report behaviors like barking, jumping, and running out the door. This is particularly difficult to deal with, because in addition to worrying about your dog, you are greeting someone who needs something from you. Whether it's a delivery person who needs a signature or to hand over food, or a loved one excited to see you who needs to be let inside, there is another person who needs your attention and care in that moment. It's a lot to juggle for you and can quickly become an overwhelming situation. A dog's enthusiastic behavior at the door can be anywhere from annoying and intrusive, to unsafe and potentially dangerous.

Dogs jumping on guests at the door is a common challenge in many households.

From a training standpoint, door greetings pose a challenge because many families have guests over infrequently and sporadically so the opportunities to train around real life distractions are not frequent enough to make consistent, continual progress. Then there are the unexpected moments where someone ends up at the door unannounced. These moments have the extra "startle" factor for everyone involved, which can cause a bigger reaction from the dogs. This is one reason why management can be an easier, quicker, and more logical option for you.

Dogs typically have big reactions at the door because it can trigger a large range of emotions for them. While the behavior itself is prompted by the presence of the guest, a lot of the exuberance stems from excitement and happiness that the guest is there. In other cases, some dogs may feel uncomfortable around guests, so their behavior is rooted in fear and stress. Dogs who are happy about people at the door and dogs who are unhappy and nervous about people at the door require different approaches. Therefore, I'm going to split this into two sections and discuss each category separately.

For the dog who is happy and enthusiastic when guests arrive

To set the scene of what an enthusiastic greeter can look like, imagine everyone in your house peacefully enjoying an afternoon together. The dog is snoozing on the couch while you watch TV or read a book. Suddenly, the doorbell rings and chaos ensues. Your dog leaps off the couch, barking and running to the door. As you walk to the door and wave to the guest, your dog is jumping up on the door. You immediately try to figure out how you're going to control your dog while you open the door to greet your guest. You don't want your dog to jump all over your guest or get loose and run into the street as you open the door. At the same time, you don't want your guest to feel ignored while you deal with your dog! As you open the door, your dog starts jumping on your guest while you try to hold him back and say "off!" No matter how your guest responds, you still feel embarrassed about your dog's behavior. You get settled at the kitchen counter with your guest, enjoying their visit and forgetting about your dog's behavior...until the next time the doorbell rings.

Trying to control your dog while also welcoming your guest can be overwhelming.

Sound familiar? This scene is so common. While this behavior can be frustrating, and even dangerous, one thing I try to remind people is that your dog is happy to see the guests, which is a blessing. The alternative is a dog who is nervous or doesn't like it when guests come over, which can result in aggressive behavior. While this "friendly" greeting is still a lot to deal with, it can be helpful to appreciate that your dog likes and feels comfortable around strangers and guests. This perspective can be beneficial to keep in mind when trying to change behavior, whether you are going to use management, training, or both.

Management Hacks

Gates and leashes

Management can be an enormous help for door greetings. Greeting guests is one of those scenarios where the distraction can be so extreme that it requires a high level of training to build behaviors that your dog is able to maintain around guests. The training for door greetings takes time and practice, including asking friends and family to come over many times to recreate real life scenarios with guests in order to rehearse the desirable behaviors with your dog. For many families, management is a more practical solution.

A dog lying calmly as guests walk in sounds like a dream goal, but it's a very challenging behavior to train and perfect.

Behind a gate

One management option to make door greetings easier, in terms of your dog's behavior, is to keep your dog away from the door entirely. In order to do this you would use a gate to keep your dog in another room away from the door. This gate could be a baby gate that is attached to the wall and stays up permanently, or a free-standing gate that you put up only for greetings. Which gate option you choose depends on your dog: do they jump up on the gate or try to get out, and therefore need a sturdy option? Do they typically yield to barriers and therefore can handle one that you set up only for greetings?

Installing a permanent gate near your door means it's always there to use and you don't have to worry about putting the gate up before guests arrive. Most installed gates can also handle if a dog jumps on them.

33

You don't always need a narrow hallway or doorway to utilize a gate system. You can install a gate around the door to create a barrier between your dog and the door. Photo credit: Breanna Norris

If you want the benefits of a gate but don't want to install one permanently, a free-standing gate can be a great option.

I understand that setting up a permanent gate is not an ideal solution for a lot of people, however, it can be a huge help in decreasing undesirable behavior from your dog. Being able to put your dog behind a gate when a delivery is dropped off, or when friends come to the door, also provides peace of mind that your dog cannot get loose and run into the street while allowing you to focus entirely on the person at the door.

Gates that keep your dog away from the door can provide safety and peace of mind when you're opening the door.

Optimal placement for the gate depends on your house's layout. In some houses there is a room right near the door that you can gate off and have the dogs behind. In other houses, the only option is down the hall, away from the door. If you have multiple choices, you might play around and see what works best for your dog. Keeping track of their behavior and body language for each option can help you decide which gate location works best. Some dogs do better in closer proximity to the door, some do better with distance.

Management Hacks

Behavior You Want To Change:

My dog jumps on guests when they come in the house and one time my dog ran out the front door!

Management Strategy and Options:

Use a baby gate to limit my dog's access to the front door when it opens, especially when guests are arriving at our house.

Try the gate in different locations of the house.

Option #1: Put the gate in the doorway of room next to front door

Dog's Body Language:	Panting, tail wagging, but not barking.
Dog's Behavior:	Jumping up with front paws on the gate.
What went well?	Fluffy did not run out the door when our recent guest walked in.
What could be better?	I would love for Fluffy to rest on her bed behind the gate, enjoying some enrichment. Next time I'll make a Kong for her.

This worksheet is an example of taking data about different management solutions for greetings at the door. There are blank worksheets at the back of the book for you to use.

While envisioning this solution, you might be thinking about how your dog would be barking and causing a ruckus on the other side of the gate. This can be a common response from dogs, especially for dogs who aren't used to being on the other side of the gate by themselves. You'll find that many of the management strategies in this book work on their own, but many work better with a little bit of training. When using a gate to keep your dog away from the door, it can be beneficial to do some training to help your dog get comfortable being on the other side of the gate and away from you for short periods of time. One way to do this is to simply toss them a handful of small, tasty treats any time you are on the other side of the gate from them. This way your dog learns that any time they are separated from you, treats rain from the sky— so hey, maybe being separated from you isn't so bad! Any time you introduce something that might be novel or stressful for your dog, you want to start with finding the point where your dog is successful and work in small increments, being careful that your dog does not become too stressed. Some body language indicators that tell you your dog is becoming stressed include panting, whining or barking, pacing, or relentless pawing at the gate.

You can teach your dog to be comfortable on the other side of the gate away from you by practicing often and giving them treats every time.

It is also beneficial to put the behavior of going behind the gate on cue. To do this, you can follow these steps:

1. Say whatever word or phrase you want to use to cue the behavior, such as "Gate up."

2. Lure your dog to the gate and then toss a treat behind the gate to encourage your dog to head to the correct spot.

3. Feed your dog another treat once they move behind the gate. Always follow their behavior of going behind the gate with a tasty treat to strengthen the cue and build reliability.

Scan this to watch a video about teaching your dog to go behind a gate on cue.

This is a training exercise, because while using management to change the environment can be an easy fix, there are also benefits to having ways to communicate with your dog with simple cues.

The timing for when you choose to put your dog behind the gate before someone comes in the door depends on a few factors including: your dog's behavior in response to a knock and your own personal preferences for greeting guests. Some people cue their dogs to go behind the gate once their guest knocks, though this means the behavior is usually happening amid a good amount of chaos. Depending on the dog, the big feelings they are having might prevent them from being able to respond to even the most practiced "gate up" cues, causing a battle of needing to physically pull them behind the gate. In the instances when a dog's emotions—good or bad—hijack their ability to think and learn, the dog is what's called **over threshold.** This is, of course, not ideal, so it can be beneficial to put systems in place to have your guests call or text you when they are five minutes away to remove the element of surprise. You can put a sign on your door that says "don't knock or ring the doorbell, call or text instead" as an extra layer or proactive action to prevent a meltdown when the doorbell rings.

*There are many options for signage that prevent
people from knocking or ringing your doorbell.*

For some dogs, you *can* cue them to go behind the gate after the doorbell rings, whether you use a practiced word or you just lure them there with a treat. The beauty of this is that a phenomenon called a **cue transfer** can occur. At first, the doorbell rings, you cue your dog to go behind the gate, and then they get a treat. Over time—because this sequence becomes predictable—your dog starts to hear the doorbell and anticipates the cue to go behind the gate, beating you there and waiting for their treat. Even better, you can use going behind the gate when guests arrive as an opportunity to provide your dog with a fun and tasty enrichment activity, such as a snuffle mat or a stuffed frozen Kong. This consequence can further reinforce the behavior. As a result, the doorbell or knock has become a cue to go behind the gate.

The benefit of setting up a gate is that you can answer your door and greet your guest completely dog-free, which, for many, can be a huge relief. You can help your guest with their bags or receive your delivery order or sign for a package without worrying about your dog. Then, once you and your guest are ready and settled, you can choose if, and how, you want your dog to meet your guest. Would it be beneficial for your dog to meet them through the gate, continuing to protect your guest from any jumping? Are your dogs calm enough for you to feel comfortable letting them out and saying "hi" normally? The gate allows you time and control to make these decisions and choose what is best at that moment.

How to handle when guests arrive

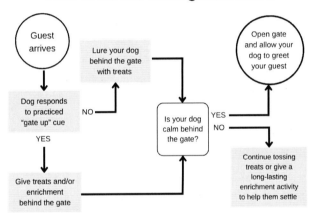

For many of the management strategies in this book, the follow up question might be: "How long?" How long will you have to keep this management in place? The answer, as with many questions in the dog training world is: it depends. It depends on your dog's age, behavior, and training history, as well as your house setup and personal preference. Some people use management while their dog is young, weaning off around the time their dog is two or three years old, once maturity kicks in. Some people use it for life, given that it is a simple and effective solution for their problems. It all depends on the dog and the people!

On a leash
Another management option for door greetings is putting a leash on your dog. Leashing your dog for greetings allows your dog to come to the door with you, while giving you more influence on their

behavior. You can use your leash to keep your dog away from your guests, or to keep your dog close enough to you that they cannot jump up. It's a step between having your dog totally sequestered away from the door and having them totally free during the greeting.

A large benefit of using a leash instead of a gate is efficiency. In many cases grabbing your dog's leash and clipping it to their collar or harness is easier than the steps of putting your dog all the way behind a gate. I would encourage you to keep a leash close to your door so you can make this process quick and easy. You can even designate a unique "house leash" for greetings that stays by the door at all times so it's easy to grab when you need it. Your dog is likely to realize that this designated "house leash" predicts visitors, so you'll want to be ready with a plan to encourage desirable behaviors as soon a you put the leash on. For example, simply scattering treats on the ground can help your dog sniff and remain calm until the guest arrives. The more streamlined a process is, the more likely you are to use it, and the more effective it will likely be.

If you want your dog to greet guests at the door with you, keeping them on leash can prevent jumping or running out the door.

There is a downside to using a leash if you're attaching it to your dog's collar and not their harness. I understand that the quickness of clipping the leash to the collar your dog already has on is an alluring part of this management option, but this often risks a tremendous amount of strain on your dog's trachea. Dogs can choke themselves in an effort to get to something they really want, like greeting your guests. While you want to keep your guests safe and comfortable, it can't be at the expense of your dog's health and physical well-being. If your dog is especially exuberant at the door, it would be better to use their harness if you choose the management option of leashing them during greetings. This takes a lot of the pressure off the dog's trachea and neck and reduces the risk of harm if they're jumping up or straining at the end of the leash. Most dogs do not wear their harness at home, so I recommend either putting it on before your guests arrive, or rehearsing the process of putting the harness on so you can do it quickly amid the chaos of the doorbell ringing.

When I was speaking to a friend recently about their dog's behavior at the door, they mentioned they were frustrated that they couldn't get their dog to stop jumping. They had tried very little training intervention. When I mentioned having them put the dog on leash, they responded that it would be "just so impractical when guests are at the door!" I reminded them that the 30 seconds it would take to clip a leash on their dog would be much easier than the five or ten minute ordeal of the dog being over-excited and leaping on the guests. I am frequently met with initial resistance when suggesting management options because these interventions are often not the first techniques people think of, and trying something new might be intimidating. Sometimes it takes actually implementing the protocol—and seeing how effective and easy it is to do—for someone to get on board.

Instruct guests to ignore your dog
Another aspect of the greeting that can impact your dog's behavior is how your guest acts and responds to your dog. Changing your guest's behavior falls under management because you're changing the conditions to prevent certain behaviors from your dog. Guests talking to, reaching for, and petting a dog are common cues that prompt a dog to jump up. If you remove these cues by instructing your guest to ignore your dog, you are more likely to prevent the jumping—especially when paired with the other management techniques discussed in this chapter. Admittedly, giving these instructions amid the chaos of the greeting can add another challenging layer for you, so I recommend relaying this information to guests via phone or text before they arrive. You could also add it to the signage you put on

your door. Communicating these helpful instructions ahead of time can set everyone up for success.

Putting a sign on your door with instructions for your guest can make greetings go more smoothly.

Management recap

Behavior: *Door Greetings - Dogs Who Love Guests*

Hack Options:

- Keeping your dog behind a gate
- Putting your dog on leash
- Instruct guests to ignore your dog

For dogs who are unhappy, uncomfortable, nervous, aggressive or afraid when guests come over

Let's set the scene for a dog who is unhappy when people come over. When the doorbell rings, your dog's response is a deep, rapid-fire bark. They might rush the door, or they might stay where they are, hesitant to approach the source of the perceived threat. Their body language is stiff and rigid, their muscles are visibly tense. If you looked closely, you'd see their pupils are dilated and their breathing is shallow. Maybe the hair on the back of their neck is sticking up. These physiological signals are all part of an automatic fight or flight reaction initiated by the fear-response part of the brain, the amygdala. Dogs who are responding this way cannot access the thinking and reasoning parts of their brain, and therefore react very differently than when they are calm and at ease. They are over threshold.

A dog's body language will indicate how they are feeling around strangers. Dilated pupils, ears back, lips puckered forward while barking, and a low tail show a dog is feeling fear.

For dogs who are uncomfortable around strangers, a guest entering the home could pose a risk. Some dogs choose "flight" and opt to stay back, barking and growling from a distance, but some dogs will choose "fight," which might look like charging at people who enter the home, possibly snapping at or biting the guest. While this seems like a big, confident display of protection, there is often a level of fear that drives this reactive behavior around strangers. Dogs who feel good and are comfortable around new people will rarely react like this, so it's important to identify that the reactive or aggressive behavior directed at guests involves a negative emotion. This is one crucially important reason why we should avoid using any punishment or corrections around these behaviors. Using punishment to address reactive behavior can increase stress, running the risk of worsening the reactivity over time and bringing out aggression.

Management Hacks

Separating in another room

That being said, when a dog displays a reaction like this to people coming into the home, one of the best management options is to keep the dog away from the guests altogether. Being behind a gate might work for some dogs, but for other dogs they are likely to go over threshold when they are feeling threatened by the guest, causing a fight or flight response and triggering them to bark, growl, and remain upset. For these dogs, I recommend offering them a safe space in another room.

There are proactive steps you need to take to help a dog feel comfortable sequestered in another room. I recommend making the room as sound-proof as possible, using a white noise machine between where your dog will be and the source of the sound (usually inside the room right next to the door). It can also be beneficial to dim the lights and create a calming environment. Providing safe long-lasting licking items, like a stuffed frozen Kong or Lick Mat, can ease your dog's nerves and help create positive associations with the space. For most dogs, getting them settled before they realize a guest is there is critical for keeping them calm and at ease. This is another reason why it is important to use a white noise machine. If a dog hears the guests from their room, it can cause agitation and stress.

Providing your dog a safe space away from the guests and alleviating the need for any interaction can be less stressful for everyone.

This is another scenario where it is important to help your dog get comfortable with being in the room on their own. If being separated in a room alone is a novel experience, many dogs will need help acclimating. It is important to practice plenty of times before trying with guests. You might need to consult with a qualified trainer to help you with this if your dog panics when alone in a room. There are experts who specialize in separation-related training, including Certified Separation Anxiety Trainers (CSAT) and Separation Anxiety Professionals (SAPro). Replacing the stressful experience of being around guests with the stressful experience of being alone in a room is not what we want out of this management solution. However—for some dogs—getting to have alone time in their room instead of having to be around strangers can be a huge relief, so it is worth exploring as an option if you have a stranger-reactive dog.

Have on leash around guests

For some of my clients with dogs who are uncomfortable around guests, part of their training plan when meeting new people involves being in a room alone when the guest comes in, then bringing the dog out on leash to see the guest from a distance. It's important to note that when a dog is uncomfortable with someone, you never want to force interaction. A dog who is using their behavior and body language to say "I'm uncomfortable with what you're doing" is making it clear that they do not want to interact. Signs to look for that indicate your dog does not want to interact with someone include backing away, growling, or snapping, as well as more subtle signs like turning their head away, lip licking, or yawning when someone approaches or reaches for them. Having a dog on leash is not intended as a means to introduce the dog directly to the guests like someone might if the dog was happy to see the guest. Instead, you want to keep your dog far enough from a guest that your dog feels comfortable. Dogs who feel comfortable will generally be able to sit or lie down, will engage with a chew or enrichment item, and are not barking or lunging. This distance is going to be different for every dog. Some dogs need to be on the other side of the room, and some dogs can be on the same sofa as the guest. You want to look to your dog's behavior and body language to decide what is best for them. Use the blank worksheets at the end of this book to evaluate which on-leash location would be best for your dog around strangers.

Management Hacks

Behavior You Want To Change:

My dog gets scared when people come to the house and will bark and rush up to them. Then for the first few minutes while they are visiting she will bark if they stand up or move around too much.

Management Strategy and Options:

Put my dog on a leash for the first half hour that guests are visiting our home.

Try keeping her on leash in different locations of the house to see where she is most comfortable.

Option #1: On leash near the couch while my guest is in the kitchen

Dog's Body Language:	Mouth closed, occasional yawning and lip licking. Ears pricked in the direction of the guest.
Dog's Behavior:	Lying down, facing the kitchen where the guest is, eating treats when I offer. No barking while guest is seated.
What went well?	Fluffy barked once when the guest stood up but she was able to redirect to a treat scatter and calm back down.
What could be better?	Next time I would convey instructions about how to interact with Fluffy to my guests ahead of time via text or phone.

One way of managing a dog who is nervous around guests is to keep them on leash near you and away from the other person. This allows you to support them with treats while observing their body language.

There are benefits to keeping a dog who is nervous around guests on leash during the entire visit. For one, it prevents them from charging up to a guest if they get startled. It also keeps them close to you so you can help manage their behavior with treats and praise. Still, there are always possible downsides. Leashes restrict a dog's ability to move away if they are uncomfortable with something. If a dog feels threatened by how a guest is interacting with them, and the dog is on a leash with no ability to remove themselves from the interaction, they could escalate to snapping or biting. A dog who feels their "flight" option has been removed will often escalate to "fight" to get the space they are so desperately seeking. Therefore, while having a reactive dog on a leash around guests is a management option, I recommend using it with extreme caution and thoughtfulness.

Management Recap

Behavior: *Door Greetings - Dogs Who Are Uncomfortable Around Guests*

Hack Options:

- Putting your dog in another room
- Keeping your dog on leash once a guest has entered the house

Chapter 7
Barking at Home, in the Yard, and in the Car

Barking is, understandably, one of the behaviors that dog guardians often find the most irritating. In this chapter I'm going over options for dogs who bark when they're home, both at triggers (stimuli that elicit an overreaction) they notice inside and at triggers they see or hear out the window, fence, or car. There are many different reasons why dogs bark, including, but not limited to: boredom, confinement anxiety, fear, frustration, and communication of an unmet need. While barking is a normal part of a dog's natural communication repertoire, the behavior does not always fit well into the human world. Humans often find barking annoying, disruptive, and a nuisance. A dog barking too frequently can start to sever the human-canine bond.

Barking can be one part of a bigger physiological response to a perceived threat.

In addition to the strain it puts on the relationship with our dogs, excessive barking can be detrimental to the dog as well. When barking is part of a stress response caused by a perceived threat in the environment, other physiological changes occur, such as: raised hackles, dilated pupils, a high tail, flared whiskers, excessive dandruff or shedding, and an overall tense body. What you can't see is the stress response going on inside the body. When a dog is barking while in fight-or-flight mode, cortisol is released. Over time this can lead to chronic stress and a number of health and behavior problems. If you want to learn more, check out Dr. Kristina Spaulding's book *The Stress Factor in Dogs: Unlocking Resiliency and Enhancing Well-Being.*

It's important to note here the distinction between normal barking for dogs—both as a species and within specific breeds—and what is abnormal or excessive. The fact is: dogs bark. Aiming to eliminate barking altogether is not a fair or realistic goal. Understanding that dogs bark as communication, and that it's worth listening to what they're trying to say, can improve your relationship with your dog dramatically. Sometimes this alone can decrease the barking, but if the barking is impacting your and/or your dog's quality of life, that's reason enough to do something about it.

Given that barking is often rooted in stress in some way, I do not recommend punishment devices or procedures, such as bark collars or spray bottles, which research has shown run the risk of increasing their overall stress. This is one reason why I love management: it allows you to decrease barking without risking the negative side effects that can come with punishment. In addition to the management techniques outlined in this chapter, it is hugely beneficial to understand the importance of providing your dog outlets for their natural behaviors to reduce boredom, as I discussed at the beginning of this book.

While some kinds of barking, like those caused by boredom and separation anxiety, require getting to the root of the issue to improve it, other kinds of barking can be decreased and even eliminated with management. I am going to break down four different scenarios that can cause excessive barking and offer management recommendations to decrease the behavior.

Barking at visual stimuli outside the house

Barking at stimuli your dog can see from the window is a common, though often frustrating, behavior.

Let's set the scene: your dog is lying peacefully on the couch. As he's resting, he catches a glimpse of something outside your house through your front window. It's your neighbors walking on the street. Your dog erupts in a barking fit, charging at the window. He is fixated on the couple as they walk away, and nothing you do or say can interrupt the barking. The couple is only in front of the house for 30 seconds, but your dog stays amped up for the next ten minutes, pacing around the house huffing until he eventually settles again. He is finally lying peacefully on the couch when someone else walks by the front door and the cycle starts again.

Barking out windows at stimuli in the environment—like delivery people, neighbors walking their dogs, kids playing, or wildlife— is a very normal dog behavior. However, when it is happening multiple times a day every day, it can become detrimental to both you and your dog. Not only does it impact your life inside the house, but barking out windows can impact a dog's behavior and mental state outside of the house as well. Because they have spent all day at home barking, by the time they head out on a walk, they are already amped up and ready to explode at the first trigger they see.

The good news is that reducing the behavior of barking out windows is one of the easiest behaviors to address with management. The goal with management for barking out windows is simply removing your dog's ability to see the stimuli that they're barking at. If there's nothing to see and bark at, there is no barking.

An important step here is identifying the window(s) that your dog typically barks at so you know where to implement management. Some factors to consider when deciding on which management option below would be best for your situation are: how easy is it for your dog to access the window, how much are you able to control whether or not your dog has access to the window, and how important the natural light is to you?

Management Hacks

Restrict access to the room with the window

One management option is to restrict access to rooms or spaces where your dog can see outside and frequently barks. Of course, this may not be an option for homes with problem windows in their open living spaces, but for some families simply shutting the door to the room where your dog barks out the window most frequently can

be an easy fix. You can also put up a gate or foldable exer
to temporarily restrict access to where your dog frequent
This option can be a good one when you need a temporary
if you want to prevent your dog from seeing the landscape
only come to your house every two weeks. Pens are easy to put up
and take down, and can be folded and tucked away in between uses.

*A quick and temporary solution to prevent your dog from barking
out windows is to gate off the area around the window.*

Restrict access to the window
An additional solution is to put something permanent and sturdy, like
furniture or a plant, in front of the window so your dog cannot access it.

*Putting a piece of furniture in front of a window can prevent your dog from
accessing it and barking, creating a calmer, more peaceful environment.*

Close the blinds

Another management option, which I find most people do, is simply closing the blinds or curtains to the window the dog is barking out. The benefit of this is you can open the blinds when your dog is not barking, however the temporary nature of this option also means your dog could be rehearsing the barking when you're not home or when you're unable to close the blinds. There's nothing worse than being on a Zoom call and hearing your dog alert barking out that one window you forgot to close. The other downside of this solution is how much natural light it restricts from coming into your home. Most of us love natural sunlight, so having to eliminate that for most or all of the day is not an ideal solution. The exception to this would be if you had shades that can go both up and down so you could have the shades cover the bottom half of the window while letting sunlight in the top half.

Some modern shades allow you to cover the bottom half of the window so your dog cannot see out, but sunlight can still come in through the top.

Window film

This brings us to my favorite solution for barking out windows: window film. Window film is a temporary translucent film that sticks on to your windows. It's easy to apply and it's easy to take off. It allows most light to come in, but it decreases what stimuli your dog can see. Some close-up shapes and shadows are still distinguishable through the film, but for most dogs it decreases visibility significantly, nearly eliminating the visual triggers that cause dogs to bark. Another benefit of window film is you only need to put it on the parts of the window that your dog can see out, allowing you to still see out the uncovered areas. For many families, this means putting window film on the bottom half of the window, allowing natural sunlight to still stream through the top.

Most temporary window films are easy to install.

I was resistant to using window film early in my career. I was unconvinced that it would have as big of an impact on the dog's behavior and the ultimate success of the training plan as I was told. I suggested it to clients as an afterthought. It wasn't until I implemented it in my own home that I saw the transformative effect it had on my own reactive dog and the peace and quiet it brought to our home. It decreased my dog's indoor barking by 90%, making our home a peaceful sanctuary where both my dog and I can relax and recharge. It allowed me to focus my energy and efforts on training during walks. I experienced the value window film has in both improving the effectiveness of training outside the home and improving everyone's quality of life inside the home.

Management Hack	Pros	Cons
Furniture or plant	Easy, long-term solution	Requires rearranging
Pens/doors	Easy to put up or take down, temporary	Doesn't work for all home layouts, not always aesthetically pleasing
Blinds	Easy, usually already set up in a home	Eliminates natural light, forgetting to close can leave opportunity for barking
Window film	Easy to install, affordable, temporary, highly effective	Can block your view as well

Window film can block your dog's view of the sidewalk and street, eliminating visual triggers they would typically bark at.

By removing visual triggers for your dog, your home can become quieter and more peaceful for everyone.

Management Recap
Behavior: *Barking At Stimuli Outside the House*

Hack options: (see worksheet on p. 60)

- Restricting access to the room that has the window
- Restricting access to the window using a gate or household item
- Closing the blinds
- Putting up window film

Barking at noises

Dogs who bark at noises inside the home are often labeled as 'noise sensitive.' These dogs come with many challenges; both for themselves and their guardians. Common noises dogs will bark at include: people walking upstairs or in the hallway (if you're in an apartment), the sound of delivery trucks, people talking outside, the sound of dog tags jingling, and dogs barking, to name a handful. Sometimes the sound a dog is barking at is inaudible to their guardian.

I have a lot of empathy for noise sensitive dogs and their guardians. It can be a really tough way to live before getting treatment because the dog is constantly on alert: ready to bark at any noise he hears, often regardless of where he is in the home. As it turns out, the world is full of random noises! The sound triggers for a dog who barks at noises can be both random and frequent—a challenging combo when trying to do any training around the behavior.

I reach for management with noise sensitive dogs because training to improve the behavior can feel very overwhelming. Given that some dogs will bark at noises throughout the day, you're expected to be ready to train 24/7. This is simply not feasible! A good training plan allows both the dog and human to take breaks and turn off from both the training and the triggers. This is where management comes into play.

Management for dogs who bark at noises revolves around eliminating the sounds. The goal is to create an environment where your dog doesn't hear as much, and therefore doesn't feel there is anything to bark at, or at least not as much to bark at!

Management Hacks

Behavior You Want To Change:

My dog barks out the window of the living room whenever anyone walks by outside.

Management Strategy and Options:

Try different management hacks to block her view of outside:
- Close the blinds
- Window Film
- Furniture/plant
- Pens, gates, or doors

Option #1: Closing the blinds

Dog's Body Language:	Ears pricked occasionally when she heard something, relaxed face and tail.
Dog's Behavior:	Lying down or resting on her bed away from the window.
What went well?	Fido didn't bark half as much as she usually does throughout the day!
What could be better?	I forgot to close the blinds later in the day and Fido barked during my Zoom meeting.

Management Hacks

Turn on the TV or radio

One of the most simple and doable options for managing this behavior is playing the TV or radio. Any additional non-aversive noise in the environment that drowns out the sounds of the surrounding environment can be helpful. I will often play classical music when

I'm working on my laptop if my dog is extra sensitive to noises that day. The same way some people choose to leave the radio or TV on for their dogs when they leave the house in order to prevent the environment from being too quiet, you can use these everyday options to prevent your dog from barking at noises.

Play music
The addition of smart home devices in many houses has made this option easier for dog guardians. "Alexa, play classical music!" is a quick and easy way to turn on calming music for your dog. There is even a selection of classical music called *Through a Dog's Ear* that was researched and developed by a veterinary neurologist to not only cover up outside noises, but to also relax a dog's nervous system.

Use white noise
When it comes to ways of drowning out outside noises, I've found white noise to be the most effective. In addition to being helpful in blocking out sounds, white noise machines are also easy to get and move around where needed almost anywhere in your home. A white noise machine is portable, small, and relatively discrete. You can find them at an affordable price as well.

*Putting a white noise machine by your home's door helps
to drown out sounds from the sidewalk and street.*

The best place to put a white noise machine is between where your dog spends time and the source of the noise. For example: if you live in an apartment, putting a white noise machine right next to the door can be effective for drowning out hallway sounds. In a house, if your dog barks at dog tag jingles from the front sidewalk, and your white noise machine is on in a back room, the noise machine is likely not doing much. Strategic placement can go a long way.

Placing the noise machine between where your dog spends time and the source of the noise will be most effective for blocking out sounds.

White noise machines come in different shapes, sizes, and colors, so you can find one that works best for your home.

Set up a box fan

In some cases, instead of a white noise machine, a box fan can successfully drown out sounds. I know I love a good high-powered fan to help me sleep at night. I would be less inclined to use this option if I could not directly supervise, given the risk of injury if the dog somehow came into contact with the fan, but if you're able to use it safely around your dog, a box fan can be a highly effective option.

I do want to note that while barking at some noises is usually normal for a dog, extreme noise sensitivity and constant hypervigilance is not. Noise sensitivity has been linked to pain in dogs, which underscores the importance of getting your dog assessed medically when challenging behavior issues show up. These management techniques can provide a lot of peace for noise sensitive dogs and their guardians, but if you're finding your dog is still on edge despite the management, you might consider talking to your veterinarian and a qualified trainer.

Of course there are dogs who bark at both noises and stimuli they see outside. In fact, it's common for dogs who can be reactive under one set of circumstances to also be reactive in others. If this is the case with your dog, you will likely see more success if you use multiple management techniques at once. For example, putting up window film and also using a white noise machine. Don't hesitate to try combining different strategies, especially if you're dealing with multiple challenging behaviors.

Management Recap

Behavior: *Barking at Noises Inside the House*

Hack Options:

- Turn on the TV or radio
- Play music
- Use a white noise machine
- Set up a box fan

Barking from the yard/deck/patio

Barking when outside in a yard or on a deck is tricky for all sorts of reasons. Letting your dog outside for short periods of time may seem like a good opportunity to let them sniff, sunbathe, or stretch their legs, however, this time often gets interrupted when the dog starts barking at something outside of the yard, deck, or patio. Some dogs get so worked up when barking at a trigger that nothing can divert their attention away. Many times there is **barrier frustration** at play here: a phenomenon that occurs when a dog is stuck on one side of a physical barrier and cannot access what they are barking at, like when they're at the fence line of their yard or deck barking at dogs passing by. Their barking and lunging reactions may be much worse than if they were on leash or in an open area with the trigger.

Being in the yard or on the deck presents many opportunities for barking at triggers that a dog sees or hears.

Yards, decks, and patios are open spaces where we have very little control of what goes on directly outside of them. Due to these factors, the only management we can recommend are changes inside the space to reduce what your dog can see, and therefore what your dog can bark at. These changes are unlikely to eliminate the barking completely, especially if a dog is barking at noises. Unlike indoors where sound machines can make a big difference, there are not many outdoor options that are likely to reduce noise triggers.

Management Hacks

Cover your fence
To reduce visual triggers, I recommend covering your fencing. This is especially important if you have wide spaces in your barrier or railing. Even privacy fences can come with gaps in the boards or small holes that allow your dog to notice triggers on the other side. Therefore, it's important to cover any openings that your dog might be able to see through.

Use landscaping fabric or privacy screen

One easy option for coverage is thick landscaping fabric that is meant to go under mulch. This black fabric is lightweight and opaque, blocking most visuals. It's also a relatively affordable option. Similarly, you could opt to use a privacy screen for coverage. Privacy screens come in varying colors. A privacy screen would be a more heavy duty, and likely more expensive, option than landscaping fabric. Be sure to hang the fabric or screen securely and safely to fit your home's individual needs.

Landscaping fabric can serve as an additional visual barrier to your fence that reduces or eliminates visual stimuli your dog barks at. Photo credit: Christie Catan

Privacy screens for fences are designed specifically to reduce how much you can see in or out of the yard. They come with reinforced holes for installation.

Use faux plant privacy screens

The downside of both of these options is the aesthetics. Having dark, thick fabric surround your yard or patio might not be ideal. I understand this sentiment, though I would personally opt for peace and quiet out there, even if it meant subpar visuals. That being said, there is a more visually pleasing option: faux plant privacy screens. These are large strips or rolls that are covered in plastic plants. They can look like ivy, grass, or a general hedge. Placing this privacy fencing over your existing fence or railing adds visual coverage without sacrificing the aesthetics of your yard.

Sheets of faux plants can be an effective and more visually appealing visual barrier option for your fence.

The goal when putting up additional coverage on your fence is to create as much of a trigger-free haven for your dog in the yard or patio as possible. Reducing stressors out there decreases how much time your dog will spend barking, and increases how much time they spend sunbathing, sniffing, playing, and using the bathroom. Even if visual barriers do not eliminate your dog's barking altogether, reducing how much stimuli your dog experiences out in the yard can still make a positive impact.

Management Recap

Behavior: *Barking from the Yard/Deck/Patio*

Hack Options:

- Landscaping fabric
- Privacy screens
- Faux greenery privacy fencing

Barking in the car

Dogs who bark at triggers from inside the car can quickly create a dangerous situation. A driver can easily be distracted by both the sound of the bark and the lunging that often accompanies it. Doing training while driving requires two people in the car: one to drive and one to train the dog. That is not always feasible or practical, so management is an important option for dogs who bark in the car.

Management Hacks

Travel with your dog in a covered crate

Like the management for other kinds of reactivity, options for the car revolve around limiting a dog's ability to see their triggers. The best intervention to reduce reactivity in the car is to have your dog travel in a crate that you can cover. In fact, the safest way for a dog to travel is in a crate specifically designed for car safety. The Center for Pet Safety has a list of products for travel that they independently crash test. Find the list and more information at https://www.centerforpetsafety.org/. While these crash-tested crates are the safest option, they are expensive and can be inaccessible due to cost, so a regular wire, airline, or soft crate is the next best option. Being in a covered crate completely eliminates your dog being able to see anything out the window while you are driving. If you try covering the crate, make sure that your dog still has good air flow and is at a comfortable temperature. You can put a fan in front of the crate or leave an uncovered portion for the car's air conditioning to reach.

A consideration for this option, however, is that your dog needs to feel comfortable in a crate. You want your dog to be at ease in the car crate and not showing signs of stress like excessive panting, drooling, or vocalizing. For many dogs, proactive training will help them acclimate to the car crate. However, some dogs will always find it a scary or uncomfortable experience, especially if they don't like being confined. This would not be a good solution for a dog who panics when crated.

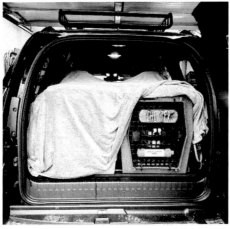

Covering your dog's crate in the car (while making sure they still have good air flow) can eliminate their ability to see triggers to bark at. Photo credit: Sophie Fitzhugh

Install shade screens on your back windows
Another option for reducing how much your dog can see is temporary window shades. You can buy window covers that either suction on to your window or fit over the window itself. While this does not block your dog's view entirely, it can reduce the intensity of the trigger your dog sees. The screen makes triggers less distinguishable and harder for your dog to notice. This solution is not a cure-all like the crate would be, but any reduction in your dog's car reactivity is helpful.

These easy-to-install shade screens do not eliminate visual triggers, but they can reduce the visual intensity.

Management Recap

Behavior: *Barking in the Car*

Hack Options:

- Travel with your dog in a covered crate
- Install shade screens on your back windows

Chapter 8
Counter Surfing

Counter surfing is a term used by many dog trainers to label the behavior of a dog jumping up and putting their front paws on the counter in an effort to sniff, taste, or grab whatever is on the counter. The kitchen is where all of our tasty human food exists. Dogs are natural scavengers, so it would make sense that when presented with an area that frequently has delicious smelling food on it, a dog would find a way to investigate that space. This is normal dog behavior, and dogs do not come programmed knowing when and where they can act like a dog in our human world. However, this behavior can be not only annoying to humans, but downright dangerous if the dog were to get a hold of food or items that are toxic to them. The best way to decrease a dog's counter surfing behavior is to prevent it in the first place.

While jumping up to see what is on the counter is a normal dog behavior, it is not safe or desirable in the human world.

There are so many reinforcement opportunities for a dog who counter surfs: the tasty snack they might snag, the object they grab and run off with, the crumbs they lick up, the good sniffs they encounter, the ability to engage in scavenging behaviors. So even if your dog doesn't actually get food every time they jump on the counter, there is a high chance that if the behavior occurs, it is going to be reinforced. This is why you don't want to rely on the intervention strategy of waiting until your dog jumps up to correct them.

The only way to guarantee that your dog will not get something off the counter is to create a physical barrier. No training plan is going to guarantee that your dog won't jump on the counter. Well, no ethical training plan that keeps your dog's mental wellbeing intact. Plus, it's nearly impossible to have no food on the counters at all times, so prevention through management is critical to prevent unwanted habits from forming, or to change an existing habit.

Management Hacks

Use a gate to keep your dog out of the kitchen

If your kitchen's layout allows it, the easiest management option is to put a gate up to prevent your dog from having access to the kitchen at all. This works best if you have a reasonably sized doorway that can fit a gate. One option here would be a gate that is fixed to the wall and has a swinging door built in that can be closed. This is a more permanent solution that will stay up for the foreseeable future. For some dogs and kitchen set ups, you could use a temporary gate that you fold up and put away when you're not using it. Some people might prefer this more temporary option that you only put up when you are preparing food and don't want to risk your dog sneaking a taste. For those who have a kitchen with wider doors or a more open layout, a foldable exercise pen is a good option. You'd be surprised how much ground you can cover with an extended exercise pen. It allows you to gate off whole sections of the kitchen when there isn't a doorway to use for a smaller gate.

A foldable exercise pen is an easy way to keep your dog out of the kitchen when needed. An exercise pen can be extended to accommodate a wide space.

Management Hacks

Behavior You Want To Change:

My dog puts his front paws on the kitchen counter to get
a taste of the ingredients I'm using to cook.

Management Strategy and Options:

Keep Fido out of the kitchen, especially when preparing meals.

Try different kinds of gates to keep him out of the kitchen.
Offer him enrichment toys, like a stuffed Kong or Lick Mat,
to help him settle on the other side of the gate.

Option #1: Free-standing gate placed at entrance to kitchen

Dog's Body Language:	Watching me, yawning, and licking lips. Some whining every few minutes.
Dog's Behavior:	Pawing at the gate initially. Quieted down after 10 mins and eventually laid down at the gate.
What went well?	Fido wasn't able to get any food from the counters, even when I briefly left the kitchen. Overall I could relax and focus on cooking.
What could be better?	Stepping over the gate to leave the room was annoying so I'm going to try a gate with a door. Fido wasn't interested in the stuffed Kong I gave him. Next time I'll try stuffing it with something more tasty.

*Even if a kitchen is part of an open layout floorplan,
management is still possible using extra wide gates.*

Tether your dog in the kitchen with you

If you have a completely open floor plan and no kind of gate is an option, there are other ways to contain your dog and prevent access to the counters. One option is to use a tether in the kitchen, keeping your dog fixed on a leash while you prepare food or eat a meal. Some ways my clients have affixed their tether to an area in the kitchen include tying it around the kitchen table leg, using a heavy kettlebell as an anchor, or drilling a hook into the floorboards. As with all management solutions, the options run from temporary to permanent.

Tethering your dog in the kitchen when you're cooking or eating can be a good option if they are comfortable on the tether.

When opting for the tether, there are some important considerations to keep in mind. A tether is not meant to be a stressful option for your dog. In fact, it's a way to allow your dog to stay in the room with the family but without getting into trouble. It's meant to be an alternative to having to keep them completely away from the space. If your dog is panicking on the tether and barking, crying, or lunging at the end of the leash, it is not a good option. To make the tether more tolerable, it can be important to provide a comfortable place for your dog to rest while in the kitchen. The tether should be hooked to their harness to prevent any choking or discomfort to their neck, and should be long enough for them to move freely without accessing the counter. Giving your dog a fun and tasty activity while they are tethered can also help, like a bully stick, stuffed frozen Kong, snuffle mat, or Lick Mat. Having someone sit near your dog so they don't feel distressed being unable to access the humans can also help them feel comfortable when tethered. Again, tethering should not increase your dog's stress levels, and so for some dogs it is not a good option. For other dogs, it is an excellent solution to reducing counter surfing while allowing everyone to hang out in the same space.

*Providing enrichment like a frozen Kong or Lick
Mat can help your dog settle on the tether.*

Set up a pen in the kitchen
Another option for an open floor plan is to use a foldable exercise
pen set up in a pen shape, not as a fence as mentioned above. Setting
up a closed space with a pen or crate within your kitchen allows your
dog to remain close to you without being able to engage in counter
surfing, which can help if your dog becomes distressed when separated. I find the pen option is best introduced to puppies and young
dogs under the age of one. It gets harder to acclimate a dog to a pen
as they get older, though some do take to it well.

Open your top drawers a few inches
Some dogs are tall enough to reach the counters with their nose but
do not jump up on them. Despite not being motivated to jump up,
their size still poses a risk for sniffing along the counter and grabbing
whatever they can find. For these dogs, one quick and easy solution
is to pull out your top drawers a few inches while you are in the
kitchen preparing food. The drawers sticking out add just enough
extra space so that the dog's investigating nose cannot access whatever is on the counter. The benefit of this option is it's easy to implement it temporarily only when you need it.

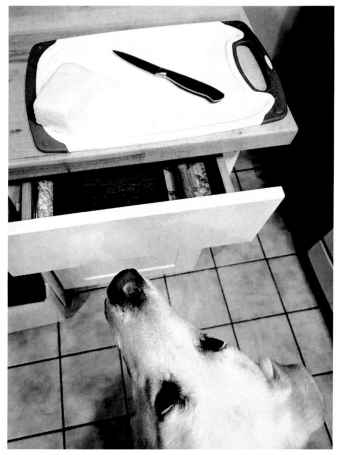

For tall dogs who can reach the counter without jumping, simply pulling the drawers out a few inches can prevent their nose from reaching food. Photo credit: Kat Heckert

Keep food items off the counter

One last tactic for management revolves around the environment and your own behavior. This step is keeping food items off the counter. This is management because it removes a lot of the reasons your dog would want to counter surf in the first place. If there is nothing enticing up there, nothing that they smell while standing in the kitchen, there is a lower chance that they will jump up in the first place. For some dogs, pushing any food that is left on the counter out of reach to the back of the counter against the wall is enough to reduce their likelihood of jumping up because they don't see anything on the counter. Even if you are doing training around counter surfing, this management step is an important one to prevent your dog from getting a big "win" for those inevitable moments when they do sneak a jump up. Changing human behavior is hard, I understand, so it might be helpful to put little notes around your kitchen reminding you to keep stuff off your counters to set yourself up for success.

Use dog-proof containers on the counters
I do recognize that the counter is meant for keeping food, so another option here is putting any fresh or accessible food in some kind of secure plastic container. For example, putting your bread into a bread box, or putting your bag of chips into a Tupperware container. This helps to both eliminate the enticing smell and create a dog-proof barrier around the food.

Airtight food storage containers let you keep some food on the counter but don't allow your dog to access it.

Having a management system in place to prevent counter surfing that works well for your family and your dog can make cooking and mealtimes more pleasant for everyone. You don't have to constantly follow behind your dog yelling "no" as you yank them off the counter a moment too late after they snag the sandwich you were making.

You can cook in peace and leave your ingredients out without worrying. It can be a real game changer.

Management Recap
Behavior: *Counter Surfing*

Hack Options:

- Use a gate to keep your dog out of the kitchen
- Tether your dog in the kitchen
- Set up a pen or crate in the kitchen
- Open your top drawers a few inches
- Keep items off the counter
- Push all food to the back of the counters
- Use dog-proof containers for food on the counter

Chapter 9
Chewing on Household
Items

Chewing is a common challenge for dog guardians, especially those with younger dogs. Chewing is a very normal behavior for dogs and falls under the "biological needs that you cannot wish away" category. Chewing can provide dogs with an outlet for stress and pent-up energy, while also serving as a good source for mental enrichment.

What many guardians don't realize is that after the puppy phase comes the challenging adolescent phase. This teenage period in a dog's life can last from about five months to two or three years, and is the tough time between cute puppyhood and calm adulthood. This phase comes with a lot of changes in the brain and body, which impact your dog's behavior. Common behavior changes for a dog during adolescence include: increased energy, increased chewing, and decreased responsiveness to training. These are all developmentally normal behaviors for dogs, though that doesn't make them any less frustrating to their guardians.

Chewing is a normal dog behavior that can be particularly problematic in the human world.

Chewing is not a behavior that can or should be extinguished

Before I give you management options for chewing, I have to make it clear that one of the best ways to reduce unwanted chewing is to provide ample outlets for allowed chewing. A client once summarized this advice by responding to me: "So you're saying in order to decrease my dog's chewing, I have to let him chew more?" They were spot on. Dogs who chew your household items or furniture are telling you they have a need for chewing. No matter what you do, no matter how much you try to punish or suppress the behavior, you cannot wish away the need to chew. Therefore, providing proper outlets for chewing is the best way to reduce unwanted destruction of your home.

One important step when attempting to provide your dog with appropriate outlets for chewing is to see what kind of items they are naturally gravitating towards. If your dog is continually gnawing on the wooden legs of your dining room table and you try to provide him with plush toys to chew on, you likely will not meet his need properly. Instead, I would recommend finding a safe chew that is closer in feel and texture to wood.

Speaking of safety, when providing your dog with appropriate chewing outlets, you will have to make a risk assessment. Chewing, especially on the harder items that your dog might gravitate towards, comes with the risk of breaking teeth. A vet colleague told me that we should be able to make an indent with our thumb nail on any chew that we give our dog. Knowing what popular chews are out there, this would eliminate a lot of options. Additionally, you need to be careful about when chewing items become too small, as they can pose a choking risk. There are products designed to prevent this now, including plastic holders for chews like bully sticks. There tends to always be a balance between a dog's health and mental well-being. How much risk you want to take to meet your dog's important biological need to chew is ultimately up to you.

Providing your dog with safe chewing options, like this bully stick in a Bow Wow Labs holder, can have a positive impact on your dog's behavior.

Other factors that commonly drive excessive chewing are boredom, insufficient physical exercise, and anxiety. These are additional root causes that will not go away just because you added some management to prevent the chewing, as outlined in Chapter 5. For anxiety specifically, it's important to work with a qualified trainer or behavior consultant. If a dog is chewing the walls, door frames, baseboards, or furniture when you're not home, this could point to the possibility of separation anxiety and is best addressed by a separation anxiety expert.

Even if you address the underlying causes for unwanted chewing and start providing alternative outlets, there are still important benefits to implementing management. I highly recommend management to all my puppy and adolescent clients to prevent any chewing mishaps and, of course, the development of unwanted habits. You could be providing plenty of appropriate chewing options for your one-year old dog, and they still might one day decide your reading glasses are a more exciting object.

Management Hacks

Put away all chewable items

The number one and most straightforward piece of management advice I have for chewing is to put away anything you don't want destroyed. This means shoes, remotes, kids' toys, airpods… you name it. The best way to prevent something from being chewed on is to put it out of reach of your dog—plain and simple. You can do this by utilizing closets, closed doors, cabinets, drawers, and tables (if your dog can't reach them of course).

Use a gate or door to restrict access

One additional option is to use a gate to keep your dog away from an area that has important belongings in it. Puppy and adolescent dogs usually do better with limited space anyway for this exact reason. It's simply easier to dog-proof only parts of the house instead of worrying about the entire space. As your dog grows and matures, you can expand how much of the house they get.

Create a "yes" space for your dog

A concept I learned from parenting experts that applies to the dog world as well is the idea of a "yes" space. You use management to create a "yes" space for your dog where there aren't any "no"s. This space is completely dog-proofed so your dog can behave freely without getting into trouble and experiencing a "no" because they chewed on an incorrect item. You get to relax any time your dog is in the "yes" space because there is no option for them to gnaw on anything inappropriate or get into anything harmful. A dog's "yes" space can vary in size depending on the age and temperament of the dog. Puppies usually benefit from a space created with a pen, versus an adolescent up to two years old who might benefit from a gated off room. Management is what allows you to create your dog's "yes" space.

Puppies and adolescent dogs benefit from a dog-proofed "yes" space, like a gated off room or floor of the house. Photo credit: Sarah Rodriguez

Many of my clients get hung up on their dogs learning what can and cannot be chewed. The client wants to make sure their dog knows what is a "human item" and what isn't. As I mentioned before, dogs are not moral creatures, so they do not understand the concepts of "right" and "wrong." So, while you can't teach your dog that it is "wrong" to chew on your belongings, you can create and reinforce desirable habits through careful management.

By only giving your dog access to appropriate chewing items for the first part of their life, you are reinforcing the chewing behavior with only those items. As a dog matures, you can slowly introduce household items that you don't want your dog to chew. Your dog is less likely to go for the newly introduced items due to their reinforcement history of only chewing specific objects—especially if you wait until maturity is on your side. This is why when a dog guardian weans off management after using it for a long period, they don't have to spend time teaching a dog not to chew novel household items. The dog already has the chewing behavior built in with proper items. This is an example of why preventing unwanted behavior through management is so important.

Management Recap

Behavior: *Unwanted Chewing*

Hack Options:

- Put household items away
- Use a gate or door to restrict access to areas with important items
- Create a "yes" space for your dog

Chapter 10
Reactivity on Walks

Reactivity is a label used to describe the behaviors of barking, lunging, and growling. Reactivity is one of the more high-stakes issues that I am covering in this book due to the intensity of the behavior and, in some cases, the danger it poses. The stimuli that elicit barking, lunging, and growling can include other dogs, people, cars, bikes, skateboards, etc., which are very common to see on walks with our dogs. When a stimuli elicits a strong overreaction from a dog, it's called a **trigger**. Dogs can be reactive due to over-excitement, frustration, or, in most cases, fear. It can be surprising to learn that a lot of reactivity is rooted in a dog being afraid, given how "big and bad" the behavior seems. The reality is that barking and lunging on leash is often indicative of a dog in fight or flight mode. Reactivity is the "fight" option intended to ward off the threat. Reactivity can be caused by genetics, a bad experience, pain, learning history, lack of socialization, or a combination of all of these. Regardless, having a reactive dog can make walks extremely stressful.

Dogs who bark, lunge, or growl on leash are displaying "reactivity."

Even if a reactive dog never escalates to biting, the barking and lunging on leash can be intimidating to others. Reactive behavior can also lead to dog guardians being pulled down and injured, or cause fights between dogs. In addition to the risks that reactive behaviors cause, many guardians come to me for help because of how embarrassing and overwhelming their dog's behavior feels to them. It can be hard to feel like the neighborhood menace, especially when you know how sweet your dog really is. I understand the challenges that come with having a reactive dog and empathize with their guardians. Reactivity is a taxing behavior issue to live with, especially when you don't have the tools to manage or improve it. This chapter will focus on the former: ways to manage your dog's reactive behavior by avoiding the triggers that cause them.

While many of the behaviors in this book are multifaceted, reactivity is an especially complicated one. The tips I outline here will be helpful, but you still might face extreme reactive behavior with your dog despite my suggestions. If you really want to get a handle on your dog's reactivity, I highly recommend you check in with your veterinarian to rule out medical causes, and to consult with a qualified trainer or canine behavior consultant. Training plans that are aimed at resolving reactive behavior encompass all aspects of a dog's day-to-day life, not just their walks.

Even when you begin working with a trainer, management will be a critical piece to your behavior modification plan. Avoiding reactive outbursts through management is essential to not only prevent the rehearsal of the behavior, but to prevent the enormous stress response that occurs in the body when a dog reacts. There is a big misconception that, in order to improve your dog's reactive behavior, you have to use every trigger you come across as a training opportunity. This is not only incorrect, but attempting to do this could be harmful to your training progress. Most dogs require a certain set of conditions to be successful around triggers, especially early in the training. These conditions mostly revolve around the intensity of the trigger, including how close the trigger is, how loud it is, and how much it is moving. When the conditions are not ideal, your dog is likely to have a reaction, and each reaction is detrimental to overall progress. Training is meant to be done when your dog is **under threshold**, meaning they can see the trigger but still think, eat, and maintain relatively relaxed body language, and respond to known cues. Ideal behavior modification plans include training sessions under optimal conditions, and avoidance of all other triggers.

A dog who is relaxed, engaged with their guardian, and able to respond to cues is "under threshold." This is ideally when training takes place.

A dog who is tense, unable to engage with their guardian, and unable to hear or respond to cues is either "over threshold," or close to it. It is unlikely that they are in a positive place to learn at this point.

Feeling empowered to avoid triggers through management is also important for your own mental well-being as you embark on the journey to change your dog's reactive behavior. As I have already stressed, reactivity can be an exhausting behavior to live with. It's important that you are able to avoid scenarios that might not go well so that you have more bandwidth to create positive training experiences under other conditions.

Of course, if you have a reactive dog, you might be thinking that avoiding triggers is impossible. It can certainly feel impossible when your dog notices a trigger from such a faraway distance that you have no time to act before they begin reacting. Using management to avoid triggers definitely takes practice. Management for reactivity is not a "set it and forget it" solution like a lot of the other interventions I talk about in this book. Management for reactivity requires proactive thinking and decision making in the moment.

It is helpful and important to have multiple different management options to avoid triggers. You will likely find yourself needing different management in a variety of circumstances even within the same walk. Your choice for which management technique to use can depend on how many triggers you have seen before, what options you have at that moment, where the trigger is in relation to you and your dog, and how stressed your dog is.

On the topic of your dog's stress levels: there is one important piece to this reactivity chapter that directly relates to how your dog is feeling. Many of these management interventions require a dog who is still under threshold to be able and willing eat treats in the presence of a trigger in order for the technique to be effective. One of the most common complaints I hear from reactive dog guardians is that their dog won't eat on walks. There are a number of reasons this could be occurring, the most common being that your dog is too overwhelmed and stressed by the environment to eat. This is a situation where you might need to consult with your veterinarian and/or a qualified trainer to really get to the root of this issue and address your dog's anxiety levels.

Here are some simple steps you can take to try and improve your dog's ability to eat outside while waiting to consult with a professional:

- Utilize higher-value treats, such as real meats and cheeses
- Practice desired behaviors more frequently indoors to improve your dog's responsiveness and reinforce the behavior of eating treats
- Opt for environments that your dog is already familiar with and feels comfortable in

It sounds counter intuitive, but if you can build your dog's ability to train and eat inside, you increase the likelihood they can do both of those things outside. Much of this part of training is actually about relationship building and increasing the lines of communication between you two.

A critical part of improving a dog's reactive behavior is making sure they feel comfortable enough to take treats outside.

Management Hacks

Change walking routes to avoid triggers

The first and simplest management option for avoiding triggers is to take walks in places where you are unlikely to encounter your dog's triggers. This might seem like a no-brainer, but many people do not realize that walks don't have to be only on neighborhood sidewalks. You can walk your dog in alleys if you're in a city, in parking lots, around industrial buildings, in shopping centers, or in open fields. While most guardians are sticking to their neighborhood for their walks, you could avoid people and dogs by finding less traditional routes to take your dog out. For some people this might require a short car trip, but that minor inconvenience can make a huge positive difference if it means decreasing how often your dog reacts.

Choosing unconventional walking spaces can make walks easier and lower stress for both you and your dog.

Walk your dog at times with low foot traffic

Time of day can also have an impact on how many triggers you encounter. The typical walk times for most dog guardians are before and after work. This makes the 7-9 am and 5-7 pm time slots particularly challenging in some areas. Choosing to walk mid-morning or later in the evening can reduce how much other foot traffic is out and about.

Use visual blocks in the environment

While taking a walk, another management option is to locate hiding spots when encountering triggers for your dog. These spots could include moving behind a parked car, going up a driveway, or ducking behind bushes— anything to obstruct your dog's view of the trigger. It's usually best to do it before your dog notices the trigger so you are not trying to pull them away while they are barking and lunging. Ideally, this scenario unfolds as follows: you spot your dog's trigger in the distance, identify the nearest hiding place, and use a treat to guide your dog to that location. While staying in that spot as the trigger passes, you can engage with your dog by talking to them or scattering treats for them to sniff out. This way, your dog remains unaware that one of their triggers is nearby.

Utilizing visual blocks like cars can be a great option for preventing your dog from noticing and reacting to a trigger.

Skip the walk all together

I know this probably seems like a jarring recommendation at face value. I don't mean it as a blanket recommendation for any dog who barks on walks. However, there can be instances when reducing how much a dog goes for walks can be beneficial. If a dog is going over threshold and having explosive reactions over and over again on walks, there is a chance that those walks are doing more harm than good. The dog might actually not be enjoying the walk, or their nervous system experiences the effects of the walk for hours or even days after. The built-up cortisol from stressful walks can cause a dog to be trigger stacked and therefore more noise sensitive at home, more reactive to visual triggers at the window, and generally less able to settle down and get good rest.

There is a misconception that walking your dog is the cornerstone of responsible pet ownership. Providing your dog with proper exercise and meeting their species-specific needs are important parts of being a responsible guardian, yes, but that doesn't mean it has to be through walks. As outlined in Chapters 5 and 13, a dog needs to be able to go beyond a 6-foot leash walk anyway. I have had many behavior modification clients whose first step in their training plan was to either stop or reduce walks as a way to lower the dog's overall day-to-day stress levels. Walks are reintroduced after the dog is more stable and has the tools to cope with triggers, like the ones outlined in the next section.

I understand this option is unfortunately not possible for dogs who live in apartments or homes without a yard and rely on having to go for walks to go to the bathroom. That being said, I want you to get curious about whether or not the fallout of your dog's walks is outweighing the benefits. At the very least, I want to give you permission to skip a walk here or there if you feel like your dog is having a bad reactivity day and you are dreading the walk for both of you. Instead, you could try these alternative options for exercise:

- Energetic play at home—tug, fetch, wrestling
- Recall practice training—calling your dog back and forth in your home
- Running around on a long line in the parking garage or a quiet hallway (for apartment residents)
- Driving to a quiet field, trail, or Sniffspot (see Chapter 12 for more information about this)
- Playing with a flirt pole (a toy on a rope attached to a long stick)

A flirt pole toy can be a great way to get your dog running and chasing without a ton of space. This can be an alternative exercise option to a traditional walk.

I want to reiterate that I am not advocating for you to reduce your dog's overall exercise. Instead, I'm recommending that you look at your dog's behavior during and after walks and think about whether the walks are currently serving the purpose of enjoyment, fulfillment, and exercise that you're intending them to. If you decide that they're not, you now have more information to make decisions about what might be a better option for your dog at this time. In many cases, suspending walks is a temporary management tool that, while working with a professional trainer, can reduce a dog's overall stress levels as long as their needs are still being met.

Management Recap

Behavior: *Reactivity on Walks*

Hack Options:

- Change walking route
- Walk at quieter times of day
- Use visual blocks in the environment
- Skip the walk

Using techniques to decrease triggers experienced on walks

The reactivity management techniques discussed so far have been about using the environment to your advantage and avoiding triggers all together. The options I am going to dive into now are still rooted in decreasing how much your dog notices a trigger, but they're a bit more involved and require building certain skills. The benefit of these next management options is that they can keep your walk more fluid, they empower you with options for those surprise moments, and over time they can actually develop into desirable replacement behaviors for your dog's barking and lunging.

Management Hacks

Teach and utilize the Treat Magnet technique

The first management technique is using a treat on your dog's nose like a magnet to lure them past triggers. This technique relies heavily on keeping your dog's attention on the treat in your hand. While this may seem like avoidance in the sense that it is not teaching your dog how to cope with the full intensity of a trigger, being able to move your dog past the trigger without a reaction is a very big win in a long-term training plan. Surprisingly, following food in your hand is actually a skill you may need to teach your dog. For many dogs, if they cannot get the food you have in your hand within a few seconds, they give up and disengage. This of course becomes a problem since our goal is to keep the dog's focus on the food and off the trigger. Building a treat-lure behavior requires teaching your dog that, if they stay focused on the food in your hand for a short distance, they will get to eat the treat. This behavior is often referred to as a "treat magnet," as the objective is to have your dog's nose so close to your handful of treats that it appears to be held in place as if by a magnet.

How to teach your dog to follow a "Treat Magnet":
1. Start inside.

2. Grab a handful of tasty treats.

3. Hold the treats in a loose fist so that your dog notices the treats and can engage with them but can't take them completely out of your hand.

4. Put your hand right on your dog's nose and allow your dog to sniff the treats. It's great if they start to lick at the treats or try to chew them.

5. Slowly start to move your hand, only a few inches at first.

6. The moment your dog chooses to follow your hand, slip your dog one of the treats from your hand.

7. Repeat, building how much time your dog follows your hand for before getting the treat.

You will need to practice this skill at home so that it becomes fluent for you and your dog before trying to use it out in the real world.

Holding either a large piece of treat, or a handful of smaller treats, is the first step to creating a treat magnet for your dog.

The goal is to teach your dog to engage with the treats in your hand, so they keep their nose stuck to your hand like a magnet.

With practice, you can use your treat magnet to guide your dog past distractions and triggers.

Scan this to watch a video about teaching your dog to follow a treat magnet.

Because following a treat magnet might be a new behavior for your dog, you want to first familiarize them with the concept before you make it harder and add distance. If you add too much distance too quickly, it is common for dogs to get frustrated because they don't understand why they can't have access to the food in your hand. Until now, treats in your hand have always meant your dog can eat them, and now it may suddenly seem like you are taunting them with the treat. Therefore, you want to teach your dog how to get the treat from a treat magnet. Start by having your dog follow for only a few inches before you give them the treat. Then, add a few more inches. Work up to having them follow the treat magnet while you walk for one or two steps.

When training this behavior, it's important you build it in small enough increments to reduce the likelihood of errors or frustration for your dog. Not only do you want to avoid making your dog frustrated when training, but enduring multiple errors during the learning process could weaken the behavior in the long term. Ideally, you want your dog's nose to continue touching your hand the entire time you are building the behavior. If you notice your dog pausing and backing away from your hand more than once or twice, you will want to try even shorter distances. It's ok to go back to having them follow the treat magnet for even just an inch or two! Start where they can be 100% successful and go from there.

When you are building distance or duration for a behavior, you don't want to make it more challenging every single repetition, always asking your dog to go longer and longer. Every few repetitions of success, you want to drop down to a shorter distance before going back to a harder step, asking for more distance. Giving your dog easy wins is a critical part of making training enjoyable and successful!

The goal for your treat magnet is that your dog learns to follow treats in your hand for 10+ feet. You want this behavior to be strong and reliable because it's going to need to hold up around triggers. I know what you're thinking: "There is no way my dog will pay attention to a treat magnet when their trigger is around!" You'd be surprised how reliable a behavior can become with a lot of practice. Every time you reward an individual behavior, you are strengthening that behavior's **reinforcement history**. A dog starts to learn, based on reinforcement histories, what behaviors are effective for producing a positive outcome. When you strengthen a behavior's reinforcement history, you are making it more likely that your dog will engage in that behavior in the future, even under different circumstances. One of the most common reasons a behavior falls apart is insufficient reinforcement history. Reliability often requires rewarding way more repetitions of the behavior than you would ever imagine—think hundreds of repetitions. Achieving this isn't as daunting as it sounds. Considering you will likely reward your dog at least ten times per training session for the behavior you're working on, it will take you just a few weeks of consistent practice to get started on the path to building reliable behaviors.

Once your treat magnet behavior is reliable under these circumstances, you are ready to take it on the road and use it on walks. It is crucial to continually assess your dog's ability to eat treats on walks. Some dogs become so overwhelmed, frustrated, or excited outside that they stop eating treats. If your dog is not eating outside, they are probably over threshold, and you are unlikely to be able to redirect their behavior in humane, positive ways. One option in these moments is to try to get farther away from the trigger, as increased distance can help a dog get back under threshold. As previously mentioned, not eating is often a symptom of a bigger issue, so if your dog isn't eating treats outside regardless of how far they are from a trigger, that behavior typically needs to be addressed if you want to make long-term progress with your dog.

Using a treat magnet to pass a trigger can be a practical and easy way to avoid reactions on walks.

Knowing when to use the treat magnet and other reactivity management strategies depends on understanding your dog's threshold, a concept discussed earlier in the book. When you choose the treat magnet technique, you can assess what your dog's threshold is by observing their body language. Of course, the body language of barking, growling, and lunging is obvious, but there are signs a dog is reaching their threshold well before that point. Typically, increased tension or stiffness signals that your dog is becoming concerned about something. You can notice tension in your dog's face, ears, eyes, mouth, body, and tail if you know what to look for. For example, a dog's ears will prick forward, their eyes will become wide and round, their brow will furrow and their mouth will tightly shut when they are assessing a situation. In moments like this, we might label the dog concerned, distressed, or nervous. Body language like this is often a precursor to a big reaction. Guardians will say, "My dog goes from 0 to 100 and reacts out of nowhere!" but this is typically not the case. Most dogs are giving lots of signals that they are teetering at the edge of their threshold; many guardians just don't know what to look for. Once you know how to recognize stress and tension in your dog, you will be able to more easily intervene with a management strategy *before* a reactive meltdown occurs.

Standing tall, ears perked forward, mouth tightly shut, direct eye contact, and a high tail can all be precursors to barking and lunging behaviors.

You will want to implement the treat magnet when your dog is under threshold, meaning they have not yet started to react. It's going to be critical that you start to observe your dog so you become familiar with their body language and look for signs of stress and tension. The more time you spend studying your dog's body language, the more insight you will gain about what triggers their reactive behavior. Not all triggers are created equal, and as I mentioned previously, a number of factors can influence if and how a dog will react to a trigger. See if you can start to identify what triggers cause which reactions in your dog. All of this information will help you make in-the-moment decisions about which management strategy to reach for.

Use the Treat Scatter technique

Another training-driven management strategy is a treat scatter. A treat scatter is exactly what it sounds like: dropping multiple treats on the ground for your dog to look for and eat. The goal with this management strategy is to keep your dog's head down, nose to the ground, and devote their attention to something enticing, other than the trigger. There are actually more nuances on how to deliver an effective treat scatter than you might think. The first is the volume of treats that you drop. However many treats you drop will directly correlate to how much time you buy yourself. It can be helpful to grab a handful of treats and then crumble them as you drop them, creating a pile of over a dozen treats for your dog to find.

A treat scatter can hold your dog's attention towards the ground while a trigger passes.

Focus on the surface area that you cover on the ground. The more concentrated your treat scatter is, the more likely it is that your dog will stay committed to searching. One mistake I see guardians make when they employ a treat scatter is tossing the treats over a wide patch of ground. When treats are spread out, the dog has to work

103

harder to find them. For dogs who are concerned about triggers, this time without a win can prompt them to pick their head up and look around, opening up an opportunity to react.

The more treats you scatter, the longer your dog will keep their head down sniffing and eating the treats.

I will do a treat scatter anywhere I need to when walking: on grass, on the road, on trails, etc. Some guardians are concerned about their dogs eating treats off the ground. I have not found treat scatters to encourage scavenging behaviors, especially if treat scatters are on a cue. I also have not found eating treat scatters off the ground to lead to accidentally ingesting anything dangerous. Of course, use supervision and your best discretion to ensure that your dog doesn't accidentally ingest anything dangerous during treat scatters.

Once you and your dog become fluent at delivering and engaging in the treat scatter, you can utilize them pretty much anywhere to keep your dog's focus away from triggers.

I always add a cue to my treat scatters. Sometimes it is a word cue, like "Find it!" A lot of times it's the visual cue of grabbing a bunch of treats, showing them to the dog, and then luring the dog's nose to the ground while I scatter the treats. Signaling to your dog that they should look for the treats on the ground is critical, otherwise they might become too fixated on the trigger to turn their attention to the scatter. This is another management technique that benefits from practice at home. You want to see your dog's face light up when they hear or see the treat scatter cue. Repetition of this behavior—saying the cue and then dropping treats—builds reliability and increases the chances that it effectively distracts your dog from a trigger.

How to teach Treat Scatters on cue:

1. Grab a handful of small treats.

2. Show your dog what you have by putting it close to their nose for them to see and sniff.

3. Encourage your dog to follow your hand as you go to scatter the treats on the ground.

4. As you open your hand to scatter the treats, say your cue. (Examples: "Scatter!" Or "Find it!")

5. Practice in many different locations.

It is important to be deliberate with *where* you place the treat scatter in relation to your dog and the trigger. When trying to fully avoid a trigger, it is typically best to scatter in a way that puts your dog's back to the trigger. The optimal set up is you facing the trigger with your dog oriented to you while their nose is to the ground. This allows you to keep tabs on the trigger while your dog is sniffing for and eating the treats. If your back is to the trigger, your dog might notice it before you do. In some cases, when extra effort is required to hold a dog's attention, I will kneel down next to them while continuing to scatter treats. This allows me to engage the dog, increasing the chances they keep their focus on me. At the same time, I'm able to move my hand down the leash and closer to the harness. If I'm worried about a reaction, which can sometimes be the case when utilizing a treat scatter in close proximity to a trigger, I like to get a close grip on my dog's leash without adding any tension.

The most effective and safe positioning when implementing a treat scatter is for you to be facing the trigger and your dog to be oriented to you, away from the trigger.

Treat scatters are effective before, during, and after seeing a trigger. This is where knowing your dog's threshold comes into play, because you will make different decisions based on how your dog will likely respond to an incoming trigger. Sometimes it is best to combine what we discussed earlier in the chapter—moving somewhere to reduce visibility—with a treat scatter to prevent your dog from noticing a trigger all together. I will often make this move if a trigger is going to be too challenging. I'll also do it if we've already seen a lot of triggers on a walk and I know my dog is **trigger stacked**, which means they have encountered so many triggers that they are overwhelmed and close to going over threshold. When my dog is trigger stacked, I can predict that it won't go well if we were to see yet another trigger, so I proactively plan to use these tactics.

*Moving to a visual barrier and then implementing a
treat scatter are steps you can take to prevent a reaction.*

Sometimes you are equipped to let your dog notice a trigger, which is the "during" category of when to effectively utilize a treat scatter. This is typically the case if you have already worked on your dog's reactivity and know what to do when your dog sees a trigger. However, even if you are doing proactive training around a trigger, there are still scenarios where it is beneficial to redirect your dog's attention away after a brief, positive exposure. For example: your dog notices a dog from afar and they turn back to you for a treat (a simplified version of what we want reactivity training to look like). This was a big win, but then you notice the trigger is coming closer. Your dog could handle the one-block distance, but the dog coming closer will be too much. This would be a scenario where you would redirect your dog's attention to a management strategy to avoid a reaction. You could lure your dog to a distance you know they will be okay, and then use a treat scatter to distract them as the trigger passes. This is where you want to be thoughtful about your dog's positioning in relation to the trigger.

*In some cases, a treat scatter can help your dog remain
calm or calm back down after noticing a trigger.*

Scan this to watch a video of a treat scatter in action around a trigger.

Despite your best efforts, your dog may still go over threshold at some point and bark, growl, and lunge at their trigger. This is to be expected! What's important after a reaction is to safely diffuse the situation, typically by getting distance from the trigger, as quickly as possible. This is another situation when using a treat magnet can be effective. Once you get some safe distance from the trigger that your dog reacted to, a treat scatter can be a helpful way to calm your dog down and accelerate their body's recovery from the fight-or-flight response that was activated. This definitely falls under the "training" category, not management, but I would be remiss if I did not mention this scenario as another time when a treat scatter could be helpful.

Use the Treat Waterfall technique

The last training-focused management technique for reactivity is what I will call a treat waterfall. This is where you simply rapid-fire deliver treats directly into your dog's mouth. The goal with this management technique is to keep your dog's head positioned away from the trigger and distract your dog with the steady stream of treats.

Because you are continuously giving your dog treats, they are less likely to look around and react at the trigger.

By rapid-fire delivering treats to your dog during a "treat waterfall," you are keeping their focus towards you instead of looking around at the trigger.

Like the treat scatter, you can utilize a treat waterfall pretty much anywhere you need to. Pairing it with a hiding spot like between two cars can be particularly effective.

Scan this to watch a video on how to use a treat waterfall.

For all of these management techniques that involve food, you don't need to be worried about what your dog is doing when you start the technique. You don't have to ask your dog to sit or give you eye contact, for example, before you cue a treat scatter. There are a few reasons for this, the first being that these techniques are about redirecting your dog's focus away from the trigger, not rewarding specific behaviors. Additionally, time is often of the essence in these scenarios, and asking your dog for behaviors in the moment increases the chances that they'll look around and notice the trigger. Lastly, some reactive dogs get so nervous or aroused outside that they are unable to respond to cues. While this is important data that tells you they might be over threshold, you don't want it to be the reason you are unable to use these valuable management techniques. Keeping that in mind, implement these strategies as needed, and enjoy the benefits of redirecting your dog's attention around triggers.

You might also be thinking that it sounds like a lot of treats. You're right, it is a lot of treats! Food is an essential part of improving reactive behavior, and there are ways to do it that align with keeping your dog healthy. First, it's important that the treats you use are very small. Most treats come in big pieces, so try using squishy treats that are easy to break into smaller pieces. My rule of thumb when choosing treats is: small, stinky, squishy. Those guidelines will also typically result in finding treats that are high-value to your dog, an important aspect of working on reactive behavior.

I recommend pea-sized treats when implementing management and doing training.

Another way to use treats in training in a healthy way is to reduce your dog's meal portions on days when you do a lot of training. I do not encourage having dogs work for their entire meal through training. I don't think it's fair to ask a dog to think and work while they are hungry. I certainly can't focus and don't enjoy working hard when I'm hungry, so I don't know why we expect our dogs to do that. Also, eating is a basic necessity for dogs, and they deserve to eat their meals stress-free. Regular training can be stressful, but especially reactivity training. When an animal's only way to get their basic need of eating met is to engage in a challenging and stressful activity, I think we create a lot of unnecessary conflict for the animal. Those are not the conditions I want to create for my learners, so I do not recommend it. Instead, I still give the dog their regular meal, just a smaller amount and use the rest of those calories for training.

I mentioned earlier in this chapter that these training-focused management techniques have the potential to develop into desirable behaviors that replace barking and lunging. Right now you are using these techniques to redirect your dog's attention away from the trigger to reduce the likelihood of a reaction. You are essentially distracting your dog. However, dogs are always learning, whether we are intentionally teaching them something or not. This works to our advantage in this scenario. When you implement a treat magnet, scatter, or waterfall, the behaviors that are occurring right before and during your dog eating treats are likely being reinforced. This means they are more likely to occur in the future. Behaviors you will typically see with these management techniques include: orienting towards you, walking next to you, and being quiet. You'll likely notice these behaviors occurring more often as you continue to implement the management techniques. It's common for dogs to start offering these behaviors even without being prompted. This happens over a long period of time (sometimes months to years) and depends on a number of factors, but it's one huge benefit to implementing these management options.

Implementing management allows your dog to rehearse and develop the behavior of walking close to you and orienting to you around triggers.

Management Recap

Behavior: *Reactivity on Walks*

Hack Options:

- Treat Magnet
- Treat Scatter
- Treat Waterfall

Chapter 11
Destructive Behavior in Your Yard

Most dog guardians are grateful to have a yard so their dog can freely play, exercise, and go to the bathroom. However, that gratitude often stops short when the dog starts wreaking havoc on the landscape. It's common for dogs to dig in the yard, tear up grass, stomp through flowers, and chomp on plants and sticks. All of these behaviors fall under the category of "normal dog behaviors" and are a perfect example of where the dog and human worlds collide.

Digging is a normal dog behavior that is not always compatible with the human world. Photo credit: Katrina Drake

In this chapter, we're going to discuss ways to protect your yard, but this is definitely a category where you will want to manage expectations. It's important to keep in mind what needs your dog is trying to fulfill when they engage in destructive behaviors outside. As mentioned many times before, you cannot mute your dog's needs. The biological necessity to engage in those natural behaviors will be there regardless of how you try to prevent the behavior in your yard. So, what's important is that while you set up management to protect your yard, you also brainstorm ways to provide your dog with appropriate outlets for their behavior.

Managing your dog's need to dig, chew on plants, and other possible undesirable behaviors in the yard

Before jumping into management solutions, I'm going to touch on more appropriate and ideal ways to meet your dog's needs outside. Let's start with the behavior of digging. While digging is a common dog behavior, it can be particularly frustrating for dog guardians. It can sometimes even be dangerous if your dog is leaving holes in your yard that can pose a risk for a person to twist their ankle in. One of the most popular options for fulfilling a dog's need to dig is to provide them with a digging space where they are free to dig as much as they want. For some people this is a section of the yard where they don't mind the dog digging. Another option is to get a sandbox that serves as your dog's digging space. The goal for either of these options is to heavily reinforce your dog's digging in these spots by hiding their toys there, giving them attention when they dig there, and in some cases even rewarding them with treats when they dig in the designated spot. When you reinforce your dog for digging where you want them to, and you restrict access to their other spots using management, you can create a behavior outlet that works for everyone.

A dog-dedicated sandbox can be a great outlet for your dog's need to dig.

For dogs who chew on plants and trees, you will want to provide alternative objects for them to chew on. You might be thinking that you already have their toys and balls outside, and they'd prefer the plants. This could be the case! The act of finding the perfect stick and chewing and pulling on it to get it off the bush can be really enriching for some dogs. You will need to figure out a way to replicate this excitement with whatever alternative activity you opt for. Sometimes, if you find sticks and then use them to play with your dog, that game can replace the unwanted plant destruction. You can also gather a pile of sticks your dog can find and chew on and encourage your dog to "steal" those to chew on. For some dogs, they like the feeling of pulling on branches to try to get it off the plant, so you need to figure out how to replicate that tugging activity. When we have an unwanted behavior, it's important to really try to figure out what the function of that behavior is so that you can use that reinforcer effectively for an alternative behavior. Otherwise, you could be wasting your time trying to implement a different behavior outlet that will never fully satisfy the one your dog is trying to engage in.

Once you figure out alternative ways to meet your dog's play and exercise needs outside, it will be important to implement management. Preventing the rehearsal of the unwanted behavior through management will be critical to increasing the chances your dog engages with the replacement behavior outlet. For example, if you are trying to get your dog to dig in the new sandbox you bought them, but they still have access to their favorite mulch pile, they will likely still choose the unwanted area.

Management Hacks

Garden fencing

A common and effective management solution for yards is garden fencing. This temporary, easy-to-install fencing can be found at most gardening centers. It usually comes in panels and you can stick it in the ground yourself, putting it wherever you think would be helpful. The fencing is typically on the shorter side—below knee-height for humans. For some dogs, regardless of size, this short fence will do the trick in keeping them out of certain areas. For other dogs, this short fencing will be no problem for them to hop right over, but there are some taller garden fencing options out there. A lot of times having the barrier there will reduce the behavior, even if it doesn't completely eliminate it, because it adds an extra obstacle for the dog when they're on their way to engage in destructive behaviors.

Adding a barrier between your dog and your plants using garden fencing can reduce your dog's access to areas you don't want them to destroy. Garden fencing comes in different shapes, sizes, and designs.

Protection netting

You can also try using the plastic netting that is recommended for keeping deer from eating landscaping. This lightweight netting covers plants and protects them but does not squish them or reduce their sunlight. This option comes with the risk of your dog getting tangled in the netting, so I would only recommend this if you are always outside with your dog supervising them 100% of the time. If you are typically outside with your dog, this could be a great additional barrier, paired with the garden fencing, for keeping your dog away from your plants. I also want to acknowledge that traditional garden netting presents dangers to wildlife. Be sure to check your netting every day to make sure no critters have gotten stuck, and, better yet, use wildlife-safe netting that has larger holes and is less of a tangle risk.

Netting can add a layer of protection to plants or bushes.

As is the case with many management solutions, a physical barrier is simply going to be your most effective option when it comes to protecting your yard. The nice thing about these management solutions is they are temporary. As your dog ages and matures, you might find that they are less inclined to be destructive in your yard. You can start to wean off how much management you use, slowly taking down the fencing and seeing if your dog continues to ignore your plants. If the behavior resurges, you can put the fencing back up. Simple, easy, and effective.

Management Recap

Behavior: *Destructive Behaviors in Your Yard*

Hack Options:

- Garden fencing
- Wildlife-safe protection netting

Chapter 12
Coming When Called

Dogs coming when called, referred to as "recall" in the training world, is an important aspect of ensuring our dogs' safety. While most people use recall to get their dog to come over so they can leash up and leave the park, it can be a life-saving behavior if a dog gets loose or runs near a road. Individual dogs have varying degrees of comfort in terms of how far they will stray from their humans. Because of this, some dogs will naturally respond to being called and therefore don't need much training, but this is rare. More often, dogs are thrilled to enjoy the freedom that comes with being off leash, and their behavior reflects this. Due to lack of training, many dogs simply don't understand what a guardian wants when the dog hears the recall cue. It's also common for dogs to find the environment much more exciting than whatever consequence occurs when the human calls, impacting the dog's likelihood of responding to the cue.

Building a strong recall through training and management
Unlike most of the other problem behaviors we have discussed, management alone cannot provide the security you and your dog need while outside with your dog off-leash. Training is a huge part of getting a dog to come when called. A strong, reliable recall that holds up around distractions takes months, if not longer, to build. Even then, maintenance training is always required because the conditions in which we call our dogs to us are constantly changing. It's not impossible, it just takes time. If you are interested in improving your dog's ability to come when you call them, I highly recommend you look into the books in my Recommended Reading section, including *Rocket Recall: Unleash Your Dog's Desire to Return to You*

through Motivation-Based Training by Simone Mueller. When positive reinforcement techniques are used correctly, you can build a snappy, enthusiastic recall cue with your dog.

It is possible to teach your dog to come to you enthusiastically when you call them by using positive reinforcement techniques.

Reliably coming when called is a prerequisite for a dog being able to be safely off-leash. This is not only for the dog's safety, but also for the safety of anyone else on the trail or at the park—especially if the area is not a designated off-leash space. You never know the temperament of other dogs you come across, and you never know how a person will react if your dog runs up to them. Not being able to call your dog back to you when you're around strange people and dogs poses huge safety and liability risks. For this reason, I do not typically advise letting a dog off leash until their recall is strong and reliable more than 95% of the time (I say most of the time because no living being's behavior is guaranteed to be predictable 100% of the time).

Waiting to let your dog off leash until they have a strong recall behavior poses a challenge because most dogs have a biological need to run and explore. This is a need regardless of age, but it is especially true for dogs under three years old. Adolescent dogs will often have energy levels that cannot be satiated with a regular neighborhood walk on a standard leash. A lack of appropriate exercise can be a huge contributing factor to behavior issues. Physical exercise is best when it is enriching in other ways and is not strictly running. For example, relying on having a dog run on a treadmill or alongside a bike as their only form of exercise can create super-athletes, plus you want to be careful about what surfaces your dog is running on and for how long when their growth plates are still developing. The dogs become more and more fit, requiring more exercise to satisfy their needs. Instead, I generally like to recommend exercise that involves a dog moving freely while also sniffing and exploring. For a dog with a well-trained recall, this can look like running off leash in a field, park, or on a trail. It can also look like a dog playing with other dogs, if the dog is social and enjoys that. Being able to run freely, stretch their legs, and get their heart rate up is an important part of being a dog.

Getting to run around and move freely is a need that every dog has.

Management Hacks

Use a long line

In order to provide your dog with outlets to run before they have a fully trained recall, you will need to use management, the main tool being a long line. A long line is a leash that is at least 15 feet long but, ideally 20 feet or longer. A long line allows your dog much more freedom than a standard six-foot leash, without the risks that come with being completely off leash. Dogs can run, explore, and play on long lines, replicating a lot of what they would get to do if they were completely off leash.

Long lines can provide dogs with safe opportunities to run and have fun.
Photo credits: Maia Perez and Alisa Healy

There are a few logistical factors that impact how safe and easy a long line is to use. The material of the long line you use matters. Years ago when I started training, we were all using long lines made out of the standard nylon material used to create leashes. Now the material biothane is very popular and has made long lines much easier to handle. Biothane's rubbery texture slides easily through grass and around objects. Plus, it's waterproof so it's very easy to clean. Biothane is a sturdy material that can endure hundreds of pounds of pressure before breaking, so it's a safe option for any size dog.

Leashes made of biothane are easier to use and clean.

Being able to handle a long line is critical in order to use it safely and effectively. You want to make sure you are not letting the leash get tangled or wrapping it tightly around your hand. It's also important that you are able to shorten and lengthen the leash quickly. One popular way of holding a long line is to loop your thumb through the handle, and then folding the leash loops into your hand like a figure-eight. This allows you to release one loop at a time to make the leash longer, or to fold one loop in to make it shorter.

Grab your long line and loop the handle over your thumb.

Fold about two feet of loop across your palm, creating a figure-eight shape.

Once all wrapped up, your long line will fit in your hand in a figure-eight shape. You can release one loop at a time to give your dog more or less length.

Scan this to watch a video demonstrating this long line handling technique.

Figuring out the best way to handle your dog's long line is an important step for ease of use, but once you become fluent at it, using a long line opens up a world of options for your dog's exercise and enrichment needs. Your dog can run and explore ahead of you on a hiking trail, or they can make use of an empty field and cover a lot of ground. Because your dog is on a leash, it's less of an issue if they do not come when you call them. If they're having a hard time responding, you can simply walk up to them, gathering the leash in your hands as you get closer. If you are proficient at handling the long line, there is a much lower risk of your dog running into a situation that is dangerous for them. Being on a long line also allows you to practice recall in a safe way. You can get many productive repetitions of calling your dog to come to you, giving them a high value treat, and then releasing them to go explore again. It expands what you are able to safely work on.

No matter how much freedom a long line provides, it is not the same as being off leash. However, there is way more to consider than just that. As I've just discussed at length, safety is a huge factor. Not everyone can let their dog safely off leash for a number of reasons.

125

Not everyone has access to safe off-leash spaces where they live. Of course, in a perfect world, every dog would have ample options for off-leash play and exploration, but that is simply not the world we live in. Using a long line is very often the next best option.

Seek out fenced off-leash areas

This brings me to my second management option for dogs who do not reliably come when called, which is seeking off-leash spaces that are private and safely fenced. This feels like a no-brainer option, but like many other solutions in this book, there might be possibilities you haven't thought of yet. I want to preface this part of the chapter with the reminder to be responsible and mindful when seeking out off-leash spaces for your dog. You should pick up after your dog wherever you go, and you should not trespass to find these locations.

There is actually an app now that lets you rent other people's yards for your dog. It's called SniffSpot. This app features yards of all sizes which are searchable by location. SniffSpot has been a game-changer for dogs who cannot safely be off-leash in other areas, especially for dogs who are reactive. You can find large, fenced yards that are completely empty except for you and your dog.

Fenced spaces are the safest way to get your dog off-leash running time. Photo credit: EJ Orth Photography

Empty dog parks can also be a great option for safe off-leash time. Dog parks can come with a lot of risks for most dogs, so I generally don't recommend them except on a case-by-case basis. That being said, empty dog parks can be great! There are actually many dog parks that are not super busy, especially at certain times of day. Letting your dog run, play, and investigate where all the other dogs have been can be hugely beneficial. Even if your dog is friendly with other dogs, you want to be wary of strange dogs at the dog park—so be vigilant when you're at the park alone and be prepared to leave if another dog comes that your dog wouldn't get along with.

You can find ways to let your dog run and stretch their legs without putting them or others at risk. It might take some trial and error to find what works best for you and your dog, but incorporating these outings into your dog's weekly routine can improve their quality of life significantly.

Management Recap
Behavior: *Not Coming When Called*

Hack Options:

- 20+ foot long line
- Fenced off-leash areas

Chapter 13
Pulling on Leash

One aspect of our dogs' lives that has been the most negatively influenced by society's standards is leash walking. The image of an "ideal dog walk" portrayed by the media is a dog walking directly next to you, matching your speed perfectly and never straying from the heel position. This standard is unfair and unrealistic for a number of reasons, yet dog guardians constantly feel the pressure to change their dog's behavior on leash to match this picture.

It is unnatural for a dog to walk directly next to us at our pace for an entire walk, yet this is the standard that society has set.

The idea that a dog will walk directly next to you for the duration of a walk completely disregards their biological needs to sniff, explore, and release pent up energy. It also does not take into account that their stride is naturally quicker than most humans. Many dogs only get out of the house for a short walk around the block, which of course sets the stage for them to be excited and over-stimulated when on leash. Guardians then want to implement training to improve leash walking behavior, which is great—but training goals can still miss the mark if they are only focused on a dog walking in a perfect heel for the whole walk.

Expanding your idea of what a desirable dog walk looks like can make a positive impact on your dog's behavior and the quality of your walks together. My version of an ideal walk is one where my dog has freedom to move her body how she wants to, sniffing and exploring anywhere around me. I don't mind light tension on the leash at times, but I don't want heavy or sustained pulling. I don't typically have a destination in mind because I want my dog to be able to choose the route we take, as long as it is safe and enjoyable for both of us. Our walks together are a time where I aim to add more autonomy to my dog's life. I do not allow my dog to walk into the street or encroach into people's lawns. My goal is to give her freedom in a respectful and safe way.

Opportunities to sniff and explore on walks are important for your dog's well-being.

Although you may find it frustrating when your dog stops to sniff on a walk, consider the benefits for your dog. Dogs have an extremely well-developed olfactory sense, and they are designed to use it. In fact, the canine capacity for odor detection has been reported to be as much as 10,000 to 100,000 times that of the average human. Even though many dogs' only outlet for exercise is a walk on a short leash, the mental stimulation they can get when they are allowed to use their fabulous sense of smell during those walks is usually more beneficial for their overall quality of life than just the physical exercise from the walk. Hustling your dog away from a sniff so you cover more ground might be doing them a disservice. Dogs "see" the world with their noses in a similar way to how humans take in the world around them with their eyes. Imagine if you were watching your favorite TV show or scrolling through your favorite social media app and your roommate kept taking your phone out of your hand or turning off the TV. Every time we drag our dog away from a really good smell, we are being the inconsiderate roommate. Let them sniff!

If you're looking for ways to increase your dog's daily exercise, refer back to the chapters about visiting empty dog parks and practicing coming when called to give your dog other outlets to run and play off leash or on a long line.

Sometimes, a dog pulling on the leash becomes a safety concern for both the dog and the guardian. If a dog lunges or pulls on the leash, they risk pulling their guardian down and potentially causing injury. Dogs can also cause damage to their neck muscles and trachea if they constantly pull on a leash attached to a collar around their neck. Some people believe that you have to stop your dog's pulling by whatever means necessary, or else the situation becomes unsafe. There is a way to balance safety and your dog's needs without putting unrealistic standards on their walking behavior, or resorting to aversive training tools, such as prong or choke collars, which run the risk of fallout, as discussed in Chapter 2.

It can be dangerous for a dog to pull strongly on leash during walks. Management can help with this.

As was discussed in the last chapter on the need for a strong recall, training is also an important part of improving your dog's behavior on leash and I cannot pretend that management alone will reduce your dog's pulling. However, management comes with multiple benefits when trying to change your dog's behavior on leash. First, management can reduce pulling by allowing more outlets for your dog's natural behavior. Second, management for leash-walking can make desirable behaviors more likely.

Management Hacks

Stick to familiar routes

When exploring management options for leash walking, the first items to look at will be the gear you use with your dog, because those tools create conditions that increase and decrease the likelihood of certain behavior—more on that in the next paragraph. When it comes to the actual environment, my main management tip is similar to what I discussed in Chapter 10, Reactivity on Walks, i.e., choosing where you walk. Novel environments will likely produce more pulling behavior than familiar environments. This is why your dog might walk really nicely in the neighborhood, but then when you try to take them to the Farmer's Market they turn into a freight train. Novel conditions can be exciting and full of tons of high-level distractions that you have not yet trained around. If you're wanting your dog to be less likely to pull, stick to environments your dog is very familiar with and more likely to find "boring."

There are two management interventions I suggest related to walking gear. I do not recommend pinch, prong, or e-collars, so my first suggestion is to consider what kind of harness you use. As positive reinforcement training has gained popularity and became more mainstream over the past two decades, the concept of "no-pull" harnesses emerged. While these harnesses can reduce pulling without adding pressure to your dog's neck, there are some risks to them. The most extreme no-pull harnesses have martingale mechanisms that pinch together when a dog pulls, usually in the shoulder area, creating an uncomfortable feeling that is meant to reduce the pulling behavior. These types of harnesses come with medical risks to your dog's muscles and skeletal frame, especially the shoulders. Long-term use of these "no-pull" harnesses can cause injury and lameness.

Avoid harnesses that go directly across the shoulders as they can inhibit movement and impact your dog's natural gait.

Use the front clip on a comfortable well-fitting harness
The harnesses I recommend are meant to fit your dog comfortably, allowing freedom of movement for their limbs. My preferred design is a "y-shaped" harness that fits around a dog's shoulder instead of going over it (see photos below). I also look for a harness that has a D-Ring clip on the chest, creating a second attachment option for the leash. A harness usually becomes a management tool when you utilize that front-clip attachment. This attachment simply creates a different leverage point, putting your point of contact at your dog's chest instead of their back. This switch up can, in many cases, increase control without causing discomfort to your dog. I rely on using positive reinforcement training to teach my dog that it's way better to stay close to me, but for the times my training lapses and my dog pulls, it's helpful that they can't cover quite as much ground when the leash is attached on the front-clip.

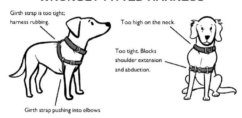

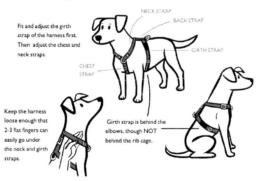

By Lori Stevens, CPDT-KA, SAMP, Senior Tellington TTouch® Practitioner Lori@SeattleTTouch.com

Illustrations by Lili Chin doggiedrawings.net

*This graphic was created by Lori Stevens and illustrated by Lili Chin.
Lori Stevens is the designer of the Balance Harness®, one of
my favorite well-fitting and fully adjustable harnesses.*

Clipping the leash to the front of a comfortable well-fitting harness can be helpful management for strong dogs or heavy pullers.

Switch to a longer (8-10 foot) leash

My second management suggestion is adjusting the length of the leash. I discussed the benefits of a long line in the last chapter, and many of those benefits apply when you use a longer leash on regular neighborhood walks. A standard dog leash is four or six feet, and I recommend no shorter than eight feet for most of my client dogs. Some even prefer ten feet. Those extra couple feet in the leash give your dog more space to move, accounting for their quicker stride. A longer leash can make walks more enjoyable for you because your dog has more room to walk how they want to while you maintain your regular stride. With a short leash, you have to stop every time your dog pauses, and the leash becomes taut more easily when your dog strays even a small distance away from you. A longer leash is one way to reduce how often your dog pulls.

Walking your dog on a 4 or even 6-foot leash prevents how much they can move around, causing them to hit the end of the leash quickly, creating tension.

Using an 8 or 10-foot leash accommodates your dog's quicker stride and allows more movement and sniffing without creating tension.

Pairing these management techniques with positive reinforcement training can help you make huge strides with improving your dog's on-leash behavior. Keep in mind, this is a behavior that takes time to change no matter which management or training techniques you are implementing.

Management Recap

Behavior: *Pulling on Leash*

Hack Options:

- Stick to familiar routes and areas
- Use the front clip on a comfortable, well-fitting harness
- Switch to a longer (8-10 foot) leash

Chapter 14
Puppy Nipping and Development

Puppies could have an entire book for themselves when it comes to using management to your advantage. Puppies are babies and their developmentally normal behavior needs a lot of managing so they are not chewing up your house or going to the bathroom on all your rugs. The more management you use when your puppy first comes home, the easier it will be to build positive life-long habits.

Management is critical for the puppy stage.

The key is to keep the puppy's world small

Management during puppyhood looks like using pens and gates to keep a puppy's world small. Intentionally controlling your puppy's environment is important for keeping them safe, as it would be completely normal for them to start chewing on or playing with dangerous household items. It also keeps your house safe. Those throw pillows you love? Your favorite shoes you keep in the foyer? Your kid's toys? You'd better restrict your puppy's access to those items if you don't want them chewed on. Refer back to the "Chewing on Household Items" chapter for a refresher on using management to reduce this behavior.

Management Hacks

Exercise pen in the main part of the house

I recommend an exercise pen ("x-pen") for all puppies, and I typically advise this to be in a relatively main area of the living space. This x-pen allows your puppy to be part of the action, but without having access to non-puppy proofed parts of your house. I recommend you utilize the x-pen any time you cannot have direct supervision on your puppy (which, realistically, is a lot!). If they are in their pen, you know they are safe and staying out of trouble. You can also give your puppy entertainment and enrichment in their pen. Puppy-appropriate chews, stuffed frozen Kongs, and licking mats are important parts of a puppy's daily enrichment routine, and your puppy's pen is a safe space to give these items. This especially helps with teething and promoting down time in between play and exercise. It's also an important piece to potty training, which I will discuss for both puppies and adult dogs in Chapter 15.

A puppy's pen is a safe space that has their toys, water bowl,
and a comfortable sleeping area. Photo credit: Alisa Healy

The x-pen can also help when your puppy is in a bitey mood and you need to put a physical barrier between you and their shark teeth. Puppies explore the world with their mouths, so it would make sense they sometimes chew on us as well. Normal puppy nipping can be anywhere from gentle gnawing with light pressure, to grabbing your pants while growling and thrashing. It's common for guardians to reach out to me in a panic about their puppy's biting, worried it's a sign of aggression. Most of the time I am able to put their minds at ease that their puppy is behaving totally normally, and we can adjust some parts of their routine, and add management, to reduce the biting.

I do want to note that there is also abnormal puppy biting. Behaviors like growling, snapping, or biting over resources like toys or food are a major red flag and need to be addressed by a qualified professional immediately. In some cases, puppies who growl, snap, or bite when you try to handle them also fall into the category of abnormal behavior. There are also times, though, when a puppy gets overtired and overstimulated and can escalate to growling, which is actually a normal response to their needs not being met. If this sounds confusing and hard to navigate, it is. There is no sure way to identify if a puppy's behavior is normal or abnormal without knowing more about the behavior and the specific puppy. If you're at all worried about your puppy's behavior, I highly recommend you consult with a qualified professional.

Management is important for puppy nipping because most of the time, excessive puppy nipping is the result of unmet needs. "Excessive", in this case, refers to the behavior being intense with strong pressure, relentless, and nearly impossible to redirect with alternative activities like playing or chewing on a toy. When a puppy starts getting mouthy, they are often trying to communicate something, especially if they were just playing and interacting with you calmly. It could mean they are thirsty, hungry, or not feeling well. It could also mean they are bored or have pent-up energy. You always want to run through a mental list of Puppy Needs when your puppy suddenly gets mouthy so you can try to figure out what they are trying to tell you.

Mouthy behaviors can indicate any of the following puppy needs:

- Hungry
- Thirsty
- Bored/pent up energy
- Need to go to the bathroom
- Overtired
- Need more quality time with you

If you run through the list and you're stumped, your puppy is likely overtired and needs a nap. People wildly underestimate how much sleep a puppy needs. Puppies require around 18 hours of sleep a day for their mental and physical development. Yes, that much! I typically recommend two hours of sleep for every one hour awake. This formula helps puppies stay behaviorally stable when they are awake. Going too long without a solid nap can cause a puppy to display seemingly abnormal and sometimes unsettling behavior.

Pen or crate in a quiet area with dim lights and a noise machine to facilitate sleep

Management is critical when creating a proper sleep schedule for your puppy. Most puppies will not sleep if there are other activities going on, especially as they age into the more active 12-16 week stage. They get too wrapped up in whatever is happening and they don't have an off switch. Or, if they do fall asleep, they wake up prematurely and do not get enough restful sleep. Because of these factors, it is not beneficial to let your puppy fall asleep just anywhere.

Using management to create a space where your puppy can be away from the hubbub of the house and can fully turn "off" will make sure they get enough sleep. For some puppies, this space is a spacious crate. For some puppies this is an additional pen in a quieter part of the house. It is helpful for this space to be comfortable and away from the main activity of the family. I recommend you dim the lights in whatever room the puppy is napping in and use a white noise machine to drown out household noises that might wake them up. Creating a calming environment increases the chances that your puppy naps enough during their designated down times.

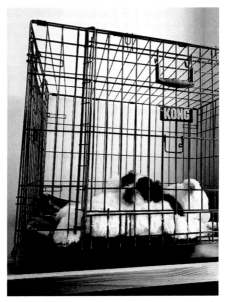

A quiet, comfortable space allows your puppy to get the sleep they so desperately need at this age. Photo credit: Katrina Drake

These nap spaces should not be used at the detriment of your puppy's mental health. I absolutely do not recommend letting your puppy "cry it out" as they acclimate to this space. This is a critical age for your puppy, and you want to avoid acute stress at all costs. Puppies adjust best to routines and new spaces when they feel safe and secure, so you want to introduce this space to your new puppy gently. Some puppies benefit from being put into their crate or pen when they're already sleeping. Some benefit from you sitting next

141

to them until they fall asleep so they do not feel isolated. If you're having challenges with separation distress with your puppy, it is important to work with a qualified professional.

Puppyhood is about arranging your puppy's environment to set them up for success at this young and impressionable age. You won't need to use management forever, but do not hesitate to implement as many environmental changes as you need to survive this challenging stage. I see the most success with puppies when the guardian sets up a lot of management from the start, because that prevents the development and rehearsal of any unwanted habits. As your puppy matures and has strong positive behaviors and habits in place, you can start to back off on how much management you use.

Management Recap

Behavior: *Puppy Nipping and Development*

Hack Options:

- Exercise pen in main part of the house
- Pen or crate in quiet area with dim lights + noise machine

Chapter 15
Housetraining for Adult
Dogs and Puppies

Controlling a dog's environment through management is the cornerstone of teaching a dog to eliminate (go to the bathroom) outdoors.
Dogs tend to not want to use the bathroom where they are living,
eating, and sleeping. Because of this, you want to create a comfortable space that does not give your dog enough room to hang out in
one area and eliminate in another. For example, a dog may sneak off
to the dining room to go to the bathroom on the carpet and then
come back to play and hang out with you in the living room. Management is used to prevent your dog from accessing an area where
they might go to the bathroom.

For the topic of housetraining, it is particularly important to mention that both medical issues and stress levels can impact elimination
behaviors. If there is a medical cause for problems with your dog's
housetraining, no amount of management is going to solve that.
Stress and sickness can also cause a regression in housetraining for
adult dogs. It is common that the first sign something is wrong with
your dog is the sudden occurrence of accidents. Many people are
quick to say their dog peed on the rug "out of spite" or because the
dog was mad. This reasoning could not be further from the truth
and it's important that, if you see this behavior from your dog, you
look into the possible reasons for it with the help of a veterinarian
or qualified training professional.

Housetraining puppies is a bit of a different story since they are
still learning the skill of eliminating in a specific place at a specific
time, but for adult dogs who suddenly start going to the bathroom
inside, there is usually something else going on. If your dog has

started having accidents inside, I recommend you go straight to the vet. Even if your dog has no other apparent symptoms, a sudden regression in housetraining would be cause for a good look at how they are doing medically.

If your dog has suddenly started having accidents inside and your vet doesn't find anything obviously wrong medically, you would then look for a behavior-related cause. Some of the most common scenarios of stress-related elimination indoors are when a dog is left home alone, when there are visiting dogs or people, or when a dog's routine changes due to a life change with the guardians.

Usually a client will report to me that their dog is suddenly having accidents "out of the blue," but when I dig a little deeper there ends up being a pretty likely culprit. A client recently inquired about help with training their adult dog not to pee in the house. This was surprising to me, because I knew this dog had lived in their house for many years with no issue. It turns out they had been spending more time upstairs with their toddler and, for safety, keeping the dog on the main floor. This novel separation caused extreme stress for the dog, and that stress manifested itself as the dog peeing inside. Another client reported their dog only had accidents inside when they were visiting friends who had other dogs. We determined this was not marking behavior (the dog responding to the smell of the other dogs in the environment), but in fact was a stress response to being somewhere new in close proximity to other dogs.

Once you've figured out the cause, it's best to directly address it with training. Implementing stress reduction techniques for your dog's triggers will be critical. As always, working with a qualified trainer or behavior consultant can be very important for long term success.

In adult dogs, housetraining issues that are not related to stress or medical issues usually occur with dogs who have never lived in a home before. This could be an adopted dog who was previously a stray, or a dog who lived in a kennel setting their whole life and got used to eliminating where they lived. Other dogs may have never learned to go to the bathroom outside as a puppy, and those lack of housetraining skills continued into adulthood.

Whether you are trying to housetrain an adult dog or a young puppy, the guidelines are essentially the same: you want to keep your dog confined to a relatively small area unless you are actively supervising them. The size of this space will depend on the age and size of your dog. A puppy can manage with a much smaller space, which is where the use of an exercise-pen is recommended. For an adult dog, I typically recommend giving them access to a room or a gated-off hallway. What works best will depend on the dog and the environment.

The goal of providing your dog with a small environment is to prevent them from wanting to eliminate in that space and to reduce the likelihood of running off and going to the bathroom elsewhere. Autonomy and freedom of movement are still important, which is why I don't necessarily recommend a crate for all housetraining. If you can find a space for your dog that keeps their world small enough to prevent indoor elimination, that is all you need.

Use gates, pens, and closed doors to create a smaller environment

I typically recommend gates and closed doors for creating small enough environments for your dog while you housetrain them. Putting up gates is usually more successful than relying on closed doors, as being a human means that you will inevitably leave the door open by accident at some point. Having a portable gate that you can prop up in a doorway is helpful for times when you and your dog are hanging out in a room that doesn't have a permanent gate. Being able to temporarily block your dog in the room with you increases the chances your dog will "hold it" while you're in that room.

Baby gates in doorways will prevent your dog from accessing certain rooms without you having to remember to shut the door.

Alternatively, shutting doors is an easy and temporary solution if you don't want to install gates.

Pick up rugs and prevent access to carpets

Another management technique when working on housetraining is picking up rugs. It is common for dogs to develop substrate preferences, utilizing soft surfaces like carpets and rugs for eliminating indoors. Dogs will often seek out bathmats and doormats when they go to the bathroom inside. If you are trying to create a small space for your dog, and there is a carpet or rug in that space, you run the risk that your dog will continue to eliminate there, even if you have made the space smaller. If you can't remove the carpet from where your dog is spending most of their time, you could cover the carpet with plastic flooring mats. If those are not an option either, you have to be that much more vigilant when your dog is indoors.

Housetraining is mostly management with just a small amount of training, so I'll touch briefly on the training aspect to increase your likelihood of success. What's most important—from a training perspective—when it comes to housetraining is rewarding your dog any time they go to the bathroom outside. If you're wanting to change your dog's bathroom behavior, you have to reward them for going where you want them to, even when they are an adult. Grab one of their favorite treats as you head out the door then, the moment they finish eliminating outside, throw a big party and give them the treat.

You never want to punish your dog for going to the bathroom inside. Even if you catch them in the act, do not punish them. Instead, simply interrupt them and get them outside as soon as possible—where you should take note of what went wrong and gave them the chance to go in the wrong place. If you punish your dog, instead of decreasing the likelihood that they will go to the bathroom inside, you risk increasing the chances that your dog will avoid you, especially when they need to go to the bathroom. This can motivate your dog to sneak away inside the house, to ensure they can eliminate undetected. It can also cause your dog to be fearful of going to the bathroom in front of you at all, inside or outside. As usual, punishment is not worth the risk, especially when working on housetraining.

Where management and training overlap when it comes to house-training is learning to recognize and notice your dog's elimination cues. Most dogs give subtle signals that they need to go to the bathroom. Some signs may include sniffing the ground, standing by a door, suddenly disengaging from play, or vocalizing. These signs are often observed in both puppies and adult dogs. However, you don't know what your dog's signals are or when they give those signals if you're not watching for them. Another benefit to keeping your dog's space small through management is that you are more likely to notice when your dog gives these subtle cues. Being attuned to your dog's elimination cues allows you to take them out immediately, preventing an accident.

By keeping your dog in certain parts of the house, you are more likely to notice their cues that they have to go outside, like standing by the door, instead of them getting the chance to sneak off and go to the bathroom without you noticing.

Housetraining both puppies and adult dogs requires management of the environment, observation of your dog's natural elimination cues, creating a consistent schedule, and using positive reinforcement for going to the bathroom outside. It's very challenging to successfully housetrain a dog without using management. As your dog learns to eliminate outdoors and can successfully go longer and longer stretches without accidents inside, you can begin to reduce how much management you use.

Management Recap
Behavior: *Housetraining*

Hack Options:

- Use gates, pens, and closed doors to create a small environment
- Pick up rugs and prevent access to carpets

148

Chapter 16
Taking Your Dog to an
Outdoor Public Patio

These days, folks often set out on adventures to breweries, coffee shops, and pet-friendly restaurants and then feel frustrated when their dog is distracted and restless. Having your dog settle in a public patio-type setting requires management because most dogs aren't able to just calmly fall asleep under the table for the duration of your meal. It takes a specific temperament, as well as training, for a dog to be able to cope with the hubbub of a public outing, let alone being able to sit in one place for an extended amount of time. Even the most stable, friendly dog will likely need some level of support when hanging out with you in a public space.

I think a lot of us have dreamed about bringing our dogs out to a restaurant or brewery with us, but the reality is it's challenging for most dogs.

There are a lot of factors you cannot control when it comes to being out in public, including how crowded it is or the behavior of other people and dogs. You can, however, control what management you put in place to set your dog up for success. I equate packing for your dog's day out to packing a diaper bag for a baby: you want to make sure you bring all the necessities.

Doggy on-the-go bag:
- High-value treats (by that I mean what the dog loves, like cheese, meat, etc., rather than high cost!)
- Water
- Water Bowl
- Poop bags
- Wipes for any type of clean up
- Bed or Mat (folded up towel or blanket works great)
- Extra Leash
- Long-lasting Chews (Bully sticks, Beef Cheek Rolls, Etc.)
- Lick Mat / Snuffle mat
- Favorite Toy (Ball, Rope Tug, Stuffed Toy)

Management Hacks

Pack long-lasting enrichment items
Long-lasting chews and enrichment items to keep your dog occupied are essential when bringing them to a place you expect them to sit still in. Common examples include bully sticks, stuffed frozen Kongs, Lick Mats, snuffle mats, and other safe edible chews. Before your outing, use a mixture of wet dog food and a small amount of cream cheese or peanut butter to stuff a Kong or smear on a Lick Mat, and then stick the item in the freezer. Freezing your loaded enrichment items can provide longer entertainment for your dog, even if it is thawed by the time you get there. Preparing these enrichment options does require some forethought and planning ahead. Chews like bully sticks are much easier to grab-and-go when prepping for an outing.

Kong / Toppl / Lick Mat mix ideas

- Kibble Topped with Peanut Butter
- Wet / Canned Dog food mixed with fresh veggies
- Yogurt mixed with fresh fruit
- Small amount of high value smear like peanut butter or cream cheese

KONG	TOPPL	LICK MAT	SNUFFLE-MAT
Mix your dog's kibble with a tablespoon of water, wet dog food, plain yogurt, or canned pumpkin. Fill the Kong with the mixture. Top it off with one teaspoon of peanut butter or cream cheese to seal the kibble mixture in. Freeze overnight for a longer lasting activity.	Similar stuffing item and technique to the Kong. Choose a mixture that your dog enjoys and fill the TOPPL with it. Cover it with one teaspoon of peanut butter or cream cheese. Since the TOPPL has a larger opening, you can also stick long treats into the topping to freeze into the mixture and add a chewing element.	Smear your dog's favorite spreadable food onto the Lick Mat. Freezing will help this last longer, but using as-is can be helpful in a pinch because the prep is so easy.	Grab a handful of your dog's kibble or favorite treats. If using treats, break or crumble them into small pieces. Scatter the treats or kibble into the snuffle mat and hide them in the fabric pieces. Reload as needed to keep your dog occupied and entertained.

If you do bring your dog to an outdoor patio, bringing them an enrichment item to chew or lick can help them settle and feel more comfortable.

You have to know what your dog likes in order to successfully use these enrichment items to your advantage. Being out in public comes with a lot of exciting distractions, and many dogs won't engage with their favorite at-home treats when out and about. You may have to up the ante for chews and enrichment items that you bring on an outing. Getting creative with novel items and flavors can help keep your dog's attention, even amidst high-level distractions.

Choose seats that will be the least distracting area for your dog
Packing appropriate items to hold your dog's attention is the first management step. Once you actually get to the restaurant or brewery, you then want to think about ways to manage the environment to set your dog up for success. Where you choose to sit is one way to do this. For example: choosing a table in the corner so you don't have a lot of foot traffic walking by can help some dogs settle. Alternatively, some dogs might find being in a corner too confined, so choosing a table on the outskirts that's open on one side is more ideal. Again, a lot of this has to do with knowing your dog and making proactive choices to help them be successful. Don't underestimate the power of this management step!

Thoughtful positioning at a patio can make a difference in your dog's comfort levels when settling at the table.

Keep your dog close to your seat

Once you're seated at the patio, another part of using management is to decide where your dog can go while you are seated. You do this by figuring out how much leash length to give them. Try to find a balance that gives your dog enough leash to move into different positions, while staying within a few feet of you, but not enough leash to go visit the table next door. Allowing your dog to have the agency to freely reposition around your chair can help them stay settled for longer. However, giving a dog too much leash and letting them engage with distractions will likely make it harder for them to settle.

Taking your dog to a pet-friendly patio is a challenging endeavor that often requires a lot of training. It's a lot to ask of most dogs. People who bring their dogs with them to these places usually have the best of intentions, not wanting their dog to stay home alone. However, the stress of being asked to settle in novel places around lots of distractions can feel overwhelming and stressful to many dogs. Using these management techniques can help. If you still notice stress signals from your dog during outings despite your efforts to support them, they might prefer staying home—and that's ok!

Management Recap

Behavior: *Settling at a Public Pet-Friendly Patio*

Hack Options:

- Pack long-lasting enrichment items to keep your dog entertained
- Choose seats in the least distracting area for your dog
- Keep your dog close to your seat

Chapter 17
Better Vet Visits

The vet's office is a challenging place for many pets. Unfortunately, due to the invasive and novel nature of most veterinary procedures, dogs can become afraid and stressed in just a few short visits. They come to associate the vet with uncomfortable and frightening experiences. The good news is you have more influence over your dog's experience at the vet than you may think.

What is Cooperative Care?

As always, there is a lot of training you can do to help your dog feel more comfortable at the vet. There is a category of training called **cooperative care** that helps your dog feel less stressed about standard veterinary procedures. Cooperative care can help with everything from physical exams, to nail trims, to injections. This training is done at home, and then the results carry over into the vet's office. I highly recommend researching cooperative care training if you're hoping to get a handle on your dog's stress levels with veterinary procedures. And the good news is that a number of books have recently been published on this topic that you can refer to. You can find them in my Recommended Reading section. Another training-related intervention includes creating positive experiences at the vet through the use of food and play. If you are thinking right now about how your dog doesn't take treats at the vet, you're not alone. This is a common challenge—one that a qualified trainer could help you work through.

Management Hacks

Choose a vet practice that understands behavior and body language
One huge step you can take that falls under the category of management is choosing what vet to go to. Yes, this seems drastic, but what vet you go to can have an enormous impact on your dog's experience. Unfortunately, not all vet hospitals are educated in behavior and body language. Having staff who understand how a dog is feeling and what a dog is saying through their body language is critical in making sure that animal feels as safe and low stress as possible. When veterinarians or vet staff do not understand dog body language, they miss stress signals and are unable to respond to how a dog is feeling, oftentimes putting the dog in unnecessarily stressful situations. Of course, there are parts to a vet visit that will always be inherently stressful for our dogs, but that doesn't mean proactive steps shouldn't be taken to minimize some of that stress.

Thankfully, there is growing interest in "Fear Free" certifications for veterinarians and vet hospitals. Fear Free® is an organization dedicated to educating vet professionals (and now other industries like trainers, groomers, pet sitters, and more) about stress and anxiety reduction for pets. Fear Free® educates about body language and behavior, as well as providing tons of techniques for reducing stress levels. They use an "FAS score," which stands for Fear, Anxiety, and Stress. The use of FAS scores gives vet hospitals objective ways to assess how a pet is feeling at any given time. This widespread education means pets no longer have to endure stress-filled vet visits if you're able to find the right hospital. Fear Free® has a directory where you can search Fear Free Certified professionals near you: https://fearfreepets.com/

If you don't have a Fear Free® professional near you, I recommend inquiring with potential vets about their understanding of body language and stress levels, as well as how they handle a dog showing signs of stress. Dogs who show any type of aggression at the vet—from growling to actually biting—are making it abundantly clear how scared and uncomfortable they are. This behavior should be met with nothing but compassion and understanding. There are ways to safely handle a dog escalating to aggression, and aggressive or fearful behavior is not a cause for force or confrontation from the staff.

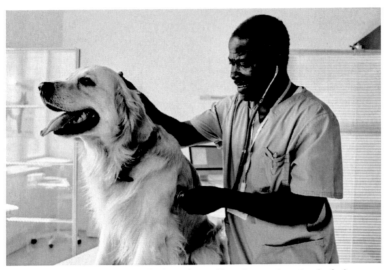

Choosing a veterinary hospital where the staff understand canine body language and stress signals can make a huge difference in your dog's experience there.

Keep your dog in the car until the exam room is ready

Once you're at the vet, one of the best management interventions you can implement is keeping your dog in the car until an exam room is ready. Vet lobbies are some of the most stressful areas at a vet hospital due to the volume and proximity of other dogs and cats. These tight quarters can cause extreme stress and anxiety, especially if a dog has any amount of fearful or reactive tendencies. If possible, I recommend either calling your vet to let them know you have arrived, or safely leaving your dog in the car while you check in for the appointment without them. Then, when they are ready for you, you can bring your dog inside and directly to an exam room.

Choose a quiet area of the lobby

If you do have to wait in the lobby, where you choose to sit while you wait can have an impact on your dog's stress levels. You know your dog best, so choose a spot where you think they will be most comfortable based on all the hubbub of a vet lobby. For some dogs, this spot is in the far corner, away from the activity. For other dogs, that corner spot would be too closed in, and they would be more comfortable where there is more open space. Even if you think you'll only be there for a minute, positioning yourself in a way that your dog can't see a lot of other dogs or people can prevent them from becoming trigger stacked, which means your dog encounters so many triggers that they become more and more overwhelmed and are likely to go over threshold. For example, if your dog is triggered by meeting new people, meeting new dogs, and being in new places, imagine the stress they could experience if they are confronted by having all those triggers stacked on top of each other at the same time when they visit the vet! Experiencing multiple triggers in the lobby can cause your dog to get overly stressed before the vet exam even starts.

Utilize sniffing and chewing enrichment in the exam room
In the exam room there is usually some downtime between the visits from the tech and the veterinarian. During the downtime, it can be beneficial to bring your dog something to do, like one of the enrichment activities for outings mentioned in the previous chapter. Focusing on these activities can prevent your dog from focusing on the environment and becoming increasingly stressed. Again, some dogs are too stressed to eat treats at the vet, but bringing something familiar and enjoyable from home increases the chances that they will engage with it under these stressful circumstances. I like snuffle mats for the vet because they provide sniffing and eating opportunities. A research study by Cristina and Aurélien BudzIinsk showed a correlation between sniffing and a dog's pulse. The more intently a dog sniffed, the more their pulse went down, suggesting that sniffing has a calming effect for dogs. If you want to learn more about this study, I've listed it in the Resources section at the end of the book. Getting a dog to engage in sniffing at the vet can have tremendous benefits. Some dogs would prefer to chew on a bully stick, dissipating their stress through intense gnawing. Planning ahead and bringing a few different options for your dog to engage in can help make the experience more positive and less stressful.

The vet doesn't have to be a miserable experience for you and your dog. From choosing what vet clinic to go to, to making decisions once you're at the visit, you have options to make the experience more pleasant for both you and your dog.

Management Recap
Behavior: *Improving Vet Visits*

Hack Options:

- Choose a vet hospital that understands behavior and body language
- Keep your dog in the car until an exam room is ready
- Choose a quieter area of the lobby
- Utilize sniffing + chewing enrichment in the exam room

Chapter 18
Miscellaneous Behaviors

We're at the point in the book where I've already dedicated full chapters to all the "big" behaviors. What's left are a bunch of smaller issues that don't require as much explanation to describe their easy management options. This chapter is going to be a catch-all for the remaining behavior challenges that guardians commonly face, and their simple solutions.

Getting into the trash

Scavenging is a normal behavior for dogs. It makes sense that when a dog has access to all the stinky, enticing stuff we throw away, they go for it. This goes for kitchen trash cans, bathroom trash cans, bedroom trash cans—if a can is open and has trash in it, I would expect your dog to go dumpster diving.

Management Hacks

Get a trash can with a lid
This issue comes with an ultra-simple solution: get a trash can with a lid. It's a no brainer, but for some reason folks still don't think to do this. Admittedly, my family was one of those who didn't think to make this change with our childhood dog, and we often came home to trash strewn about the house. Looking back, I think about how much less frustrated we would have been if we had simply covered the trash can.

Get a trash can that is too tall for your small dog
I did finally learn this lesson in adulthood though, when my five-pound chihuahua kept stealing tissues from our bathroom trash can. Not only was her foraging behavior reinforced whenever she found a tissue in the trash, but she also found it reinforcing when we chased her around to try and retrieve the stolen item. Luckily for us, a quick fix was a trash can too tall for her to reach.

Getting a trash can with a lid can solve a dog's tendencies to go dumpster-diving.

Put the trash can in an area that is inaccessible to your dog
Another possible management solution to prevent your dog from getting into the trash is to put the trash can in an area that is inaccessible to the dog such as in a pantry, with the door closed or in a cabinet, perhaps under the kitchen sink. You could also prevent access to trash cans by closing bedroom and bathroom doors or gating off the kitchen with x-pens or gates, as recommended in the chapter about Counter Surfing.

Management Recap
Behavior: *Getting into the Trash*

Hack Options:

- Get a trash can with a lid
- Get a trash can that is too tall for your small dog

- Put the trash can in a pantry or cabinet with a closed door
- Restrict the dog's access to rooms with trash cans by closing doors or using gates

Door-dashing

One of the most dangerous behaviors that a dog can do is dashing out the door off leash. **Door-dashing** is when a dog quickly runs out the door any chance they get, sometimes sneaking past a human who is trying to keep them inside. This is especially dangerous due to how motivated the dog often is to run off once they gain freedom, risking running into danger in the street or with another person or dog. This behavior can be improved with training, but even if you go that route, it will take time to build the behavior to the point of effective reliability. This is why, if you have a dog who tends to door dash, I recommend implementing management.

This is another example of a behavior where only a physical barrier guarantees your dog's safety. Training—even extensive training—does not create 100% reliable behavior. You never know when a distraction will show up that you have not trained around, and suddenly your dog forgets all they have learned and sprints out the door. Management is a highly effective way to keep your dog safe.

Management Hacks

Use a gate in the door or the foyer

The management I recommend here is simply a gate at the door. This can be a gate that is installed in the door frame, or a longer gate that creates a barrier around your door. Both options put a barrier between your dog and the outside world when you open the door. Which one is best for you depends on your setup and your dog.

A gate in the door frame will prevent your dog from running out when you are picking up a delivery or talking to someone outside.

A gate around the door can be the most effective option for reducing door-dashing behaviors. Photo credit: Breanna Norris

I especially like using management to prevent door dashing if the dog lives in a busy household. When families have kids who are going in and out of the house frequently, a physical barrier in addition to the door is usually the safest option. I don't expect adults to always remember to shut the door, so I definitely don't expect kids to. Being realistic when it comes to expectations around human behavior is a much safer option than thinking a guardian will never forget or slip up.

As discussed in Chapter 6, one option that would help if the dog tends to bolt out the door when guests arrive, is to put your dog on a leash before you open the door. If you're holding the leash as you greet your guests and they walk inside, your dog is unable to sneak past anyone and get into the street.

Again, putting this simple management step in place can be a life-saving measure for dogs who are motivated to run out whenever the door is open. Whether you end up working on training the behavior or not, physical barriers leave little room for error.

Management Recap
Behavior: *Dashing Out the Door*

Hack Options:

- Gate in the doorway
- Gate surrounding the door in the foyer
- Leash the dog before opening the door

Scratching at doors

For many dogs, scratching at doors is a common way of communicating. They scratch at the door because they either don't want to be confined to where they are, or they want access to whatever is on the other side of the door. I see this a lot when a dog wants to go outside. This communication is especially valuable from puppies because it tells guardians when the dog needs to go to the bathroom, which can prevent accidents. Even in adult dogs, it is beneficial for a dog to be able to communicate their needs. It seems insignificant, but this ability to create two-way communication throughout the day can improve a dog's quality of life. However, guardians understandably can get frustrated when the scratching starts to damage the door.

This is yet another instance where it's important to identify if the scratching is a result of panic or extreme stress. Dogs who frantically scratch at doors when they are left alone or separated from their guardians need support beyond management. The underlying cause of the scratching needs to be addressed if you want to see improvement.

For dogs who are scratching at the door to notify you that they need to go to the bathroom, providing an alternative form of communication like hanging bells can address the issue. You can find these "doggy doorbells" online and see which option is best for your home and dog. The goal would be to teach your dog to hit these bells with their nose or paw to notify you that they need to go out. Using the bells would replace the scratching.

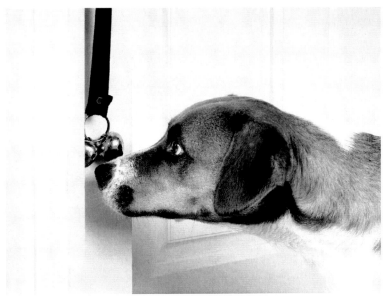

"Doggy doorbells" can replace scratching as a communication tool for your dog asking to go outside.

Regular door scratching as a means for everyday communication can be a good candidate for management. There are two different goals for management interventions here: one is to prevent your dog from scratching altogether, and the other is to protect your home when your dog scratches.

Management Hacks

Put up gates or pens around the door

To prevent the scratching altogether you need to put up a barrier between your dog and where they are inclined to scratch. For example, if your dog scratches at closed doors because they want to get to the people inside the room, you could put up a gate or pen around the door. This is another situation where having a foldable gate at home is helpful. You can put the gate up when your dog is scratching at the door, and then tuck the gate away when the scratching is no longer occurring.

Preventing your dog's access to a door will stop them from scratching at it.

Install a protective cover on the door

If your dog constantly scratches at one door—for example, the back door to signal they want to go outside—putting a protective cover on your door is probably a more practical solution. Installing a plastic cover over the area your dog scratches is a relatively easy way to protect the door.

If your dog is relentless about scratching at one of your doors, covering the door with thick plastic can protect the door long-term.

One of my training colleagues came up with a creative solution for her dog scratching a unique surface. Her dog paws at the freezer door because he quickly learned that's where his favorite frozen treats came from. Instead of doing training to curb this behavior, she chose to implement management. She stuck sheets of sandpaper to the freezer door. This not only protected the door, but it also gently filed the dog's nails any time the dog scratched. "Scratchboards"—planks with sandpaper on them—have become a popular alternative to nail trims. This management intervention with sandpaper on the door ended up being a win-win.

Covering the freezer with sandpaper is a creative solution to a dog's scratching.

Management Recap

Behavior: *Scratching at Doors*

Hack Options:

- Put up gates or pens around the door
- Install a protective cover on the door

Conclusion
Embracing a Management
Mindset

The use of management in the dog world might feel foreign, but humans are actually well-versed in using management in their daily lives. We often rely on management to reduce stress. We choose the route home with less traffic. We enter the shortest line at the grocery store. We cancel plans if someone will be there who we don't want to see. We are able to change our conditions to influence what happens next.

Humans are constantly adjusting our environment in an effort to increase or decrease the likelihood of certain behaviors. Any type of "life hack" is usually going to fall under the category of management. We pack a lunch to prevent the behavior of spending money. We set our gym clothes out the night before to increase the chances we make it to our morning workout. We put our alarm clock across the room to reduce the likelihood that we hit snooze. We leave items out that we don't want to forget. Instead of expecting these goal behaviors to occur by sheer willpower, we make changes to the environment to impact the likelihood of success. Humans unknowingly use management in their own lives every single day.

I remember a story one of my brilliant training colleagues shared about using management in their own life. Their vacuum was in a cluttered closet, and it was a huge pain to get it out to use it. This resulted in no one wanting to vacuum. One day, they finally cleaned out the closet and made the vacuum easily accessible. Suddenly, everyone's vacuuming behavior increased. Instead of expecting the vacuuming behavior to change on its own, they changed the environment to make it more likely to occur.

Whether you realize it or not, management is effective in changing your behavior in your own life. If you do it for yourself, why not with your dog? When applying to dogs, it is not "cheating"—in fact, it's quite the opposite: utilizing management is a smart way to achieve harmony in life with your dog. Our dogs are trying their best to live in and adapt to this human world full of sometimes unrealistic expectations. Management allows us to help them be more successful.

Management is one of the best ways you can honor the human-canine bond. When you opt for management, you take confrontation and force-based interventions—which could possibly harm your dog and your relationship with your dog—off the table. Instead, you will use your creativity, observation skills, and critical thinking to consider how you can use the environment to your advantage. This use of management is the cornerstone of any good training plan. The mantra "change the conditions to change behavior" is at the forefront of a management mindset.

Another part of honoring the human-canine bond is considering the "canine" part of the relationship. When you are deciding which management solutions to use, you are automatically going to be thinking about your dog's behavior, habits, and needs. This extra level of care you're taking when trying to change your dog's behavior is one step to building a relationship that is enriching and fulfilling for both of you. Society has created an unrealistic narrative around who dogs are and how they should behave, expecting them to rarely display all the normal behaviors that make them a dog. One of the best things you can do for your dog is truly understand them as an individual, taking into account their behavior and the body language they use to communicate.

The new observation skills that you gain as you implement management into your dog's life will allow you to also notice the new, more desirable behaviors that start to emerge as a result. When you reduce or eliminate a behavior through management, other behaviors will show up in its place. For example, when you eliminate your dog's barking out the window by putting up window film, the behavior of resting on the couch could replace it. Or, if you prevent counter surfing by putting up a baby gate, you will likely see an increase in the behavior of sitting at the edge of the kitchen, calmly watching you cook. Management opens up your ability to observe and reinforce new, more desirable behaviors from your dog—a helpful argument against any management naysayers.

I understand the challenges that can come from sharing your life with a dog. I empathize with the frustrations their behaviors can cause. I also appreciate the love so many of you have for your dog, and how you think of them as family. I feel it's important to prioritize solutions that benefit both parties. Management is so often that solution. My hope is that I have normalized the use of management and given you ample options of how to apply it in your own life. With the new perspectives you have from this book, you are empowered to make positive changes for you and your dog.

Management
Hacks
Worksheet

On the next page you will find worksheets that you can use to assess which management solutions work best for your particular needs. You want to start by identifying the behavior you want to change. It is helpful to note what the behavior is and when the behavior happens. Then you will identify the management solution you want to implement. For example, "block access to the windows" or "choose a different walking route." From there, you can list different variations of that management solution so you can figure out which option is best. For example, when implementing management that blocks your dog's access to the window, options could include "put a gate up" or "move the bookcase in front of the window." Or, for changing walking routes, options could include, "The elementary school by our home" or "The parking lot of our apartment building."

Once you identify your options, you will then try implementing them and take notes about what works or what doesn't. This is a helpful exercise in identifying the body language and behavior you observe from your dog, as that is what gives you information about how they are responding to the management. By using these worksheets to take data about each intervention option you can make an informed decision about what works best for your dog, home, and family.

Management Hacks

Behavior You Want To Change:

Management Strategy and Options:

Option #1:

Dog's Body Language:	
Dog's Behavior:	
What went well?	
What could be better?	

Management Hacks

Dog's Body Language:	
Dog's Behavior:	
What went well?	
What could be better?	

Option #3:

Dog's Body Language:	
Dog's Behavior:	
What went well?	
What could be better?	

Resources & Recommended Reading

Books

A Dog's Fabulous Sense of Smell. Anne Lill Kvam, 2022. Clear step-by-step instructions for training your dog to find everything from hidden treats to lost keys.

Animal Training: Successful Animal Management Through Positive Reinforcement. Ken Ramirez, 2019. An animal training textbook rich with information about training using positive reinforcement.

Applied Behavior Analysis 3rd Edition. John Cooper, Timothy Heron, and William Heward, 2019. This textbook provides additional information on research and data about the use of punishment cited in Chapter 2.

Behavior Adjustment Training 2.0: New Practical Techniques for Fear, Frustration, and Aggression in Dogs. Grisha Stewart, 2016. A book with protocols for improving reactivity, aggression, frustration, and fear.

Canine Enrichment for the Real World. Allie Bender and Emily Strong, 2019. A deep dive into enrichment and how to use it to directly improve your dog's quality of life.

Canine Enrichment for the Real World Workbook. Allie Bender and Emily Strong, 2022. A companion workbook with blank worksheets to ensure your dog's needs are being met which reduces undesirable behaviors.

Control Unleashed Reactive to Relaxed. Leslie McDevitt, 2019. Techniques for teaching your dog life skills and coping skills in a two-way system of communicating.

Cooperative Care: Seven Steps to Stress-Free Husbandry. Deb Jones, 2018. A guide for building your dog's confidence with husbandry procedures.

Doggie Language: A Dog Lover's Guide to Understanding Your Best Friend. Lili Chin, 2020. This easy-to-digest picture book explains how to understand dog body language.

Don't Shoot the Dog. Karen Pryor, 2002. For learning more about how to embrace positive reinforcement with the animals and people in your life.

Gentle Hands Off Dog Training. Sarah Whitehead, 2011. Step-by-step instructions for training basic behaviors and cues.

Learning and Behavior 7th Edition. Paul Chance, 2020. A textbook that covers the scientific approach to learning and behavior. A helpful supplement to the contents of Chapter 2.

On Talking Terms with Dogs: Calming Signals. Turid Rugaas, 2005. This book will show you how to recognize the body language that dogs use to communicate with each other and with us.

Plenty in Life Is Free: Reflections on Dogs, Training and Finding Grace. Kathy Sdao, 2012 This book will help you rethink your relationship with your dog and what it means to have a partnership rather than fight for control.

Rocket Recall: Unleash Your Dog's Desire to Return to You through Motivation-Based Training - Second Edition. Simone Mueller, 2023. A step-by-step guide to building a joyful and reliable recall with your dog.

Separation Anxiety in Dogs: Next Generation Treatment Protocols and Practice. Malena DeMartini-Price, 2020. New and improved book filled with data-driven advice about how to treat separation anxiety.

Stop Walking Your Dog. Niki French, 2021. A guide to evaluating if a traditional walk is beneficial for your dog, and what skills are helpful to teach your dog to improve your life together.

The Stress Factor in Dogs: Unlocking Resiliency and Enhancing Well-Being. Kristina Spaulding, 2022. A deep dive into the impact stress has on dogs, and how understanding that can improve your dog's quality of life.

Veterinary Cooperative Care: Enhancing Animal Health Through Collaboration with Veterinarians, Pet Owners, and Animal Trainers. Pat Miller and Dr. Leslie Sinn, 2023. A compilation of experts in the training and veterinary field explaining how to make vet visits and care less stressful.

Websites

American Veterinary Society of Animal Behavior. www.avsab.org. AVSAB provides position statements on important topics, including the use of punishment in training, puppy socialization, and dominance theory.

Behavior Works. www.behaviorworks.org. Dr. Susan Friedman's organization Behavior Works has extensive resources about how Applied Behavior Analysis works applies to training our pets.

International Association of Animal Behavior Consultants. www.iaabc. org. IAABC is a membership and certifying organization for animal trainers. The website includes training resources and a directory of credentialed trainers.

Karen Pryor Academy. www.karenpryoracademy.com. The Karen Pryor Academy has training courses for pet guardians, as well as a directory for their credentialed trainers.

Kiki Yablon's Blog. https://kikiyablondogtraining.com/kiki-blog. Kiki Yablon is a dog trainer who has a master's degree in Applied Behavioral Science and breaks down important scientific principles as they relate to dog training.

Dog Training by Kikopup YouTube Channel. https://www.youtube. com/@kikopup. Dog trainer Emily Larlham shares in-depth educational videos about how to train your dog.

Pulse Study "At the Heart of the Walk." https://www.dogfieldstudy. com/en/study/pulse-study-at-the-heart-of-the-walk. This website outlines the findings of the sniffing study mentioned in Chapter 17.

Index

About the Author

Juliana DeWillems is a Certified Dog Trainer and Dog Behavior Consultant, and the owner of JW Dog Training in the Washington, D.C. area. She began training dogs in 2013, jumpstarting her career by graduating from the Karen Pryor Academy with distinction. After earning her certification, Juliana began working on the behavior team at a large city animal shelter, as well as training private clients. Working with a diverse population of dogs between the shelter and training clients gave Juliana  extensive hands-on experience solving behavior issues. This led to a well-rounded perspective on how to use positive reinforcement techniques to effectively and efficiently help dogs and the people who care for them. Juliana specializes in dogs who display fearful, reactive, and aggressive behavior.

Juliana is also Faculty at the Karen Pryor Academy, teaching trainers about the principles of behavior science and clicker training. When she is not training private clients or teaching her KPA students, Juliana works with brands and media outlets to educate the public about dog training and behavior. Her expertise has been featured on the radio, in national magazines, on multiple Washington D.C. news programs, and on major retail and business websites. Juliana's most valued and important part of her job as a dog trainer and behavior consultant is improving the human-canine bond. Learn more about Juliana at www.jwdogtraining.com.

Acknowledgments

So many people made this book possible. Thank you to Dogwise for taking a chance on both this topic and on a first-time author. Thank you for guiding me through the process and being patient and understanding of my learning curve. I am so proud of the robust resource my initial idea turned into, and it wouldn't be what it is without the talented Dogwise team.

Thank you to Bex Peyton for spending hours helping me edit the manuscript ahead of submitting it for a contract. Your expertise surely saved us an enormous amount of time in the publishing process.

Thank you to Kiki Yablon for your time and expertise to help me make sure I convey the science correctly. I am grateful for everything I learn from you, and even more grateful for our friendship.

Thank you to everyone who gave me their time, energy, and dogs so I could build the extensive library of photos needed for this book. Choosing to take most of the photos myself was a huge undertaking that I could not have done without the help of my friends, colleagues, and clients.

Thank you to all the endorsers who took time out of their busy schedules to review this book. I am acutely aware of how much work and consideration that took, and I am so appreciative.

Thank you to my amazing team of trainers at JW Dog Training for keeping the business thriving while I have spent so much time working on this book.

Thank you to all my internet friends who, over the years on dog training social media, have helped me become a better, more creative, and more empathetic trainer. I am grateful for each and every connection I have made, and for the positive reinforcement community we have built online.

Thank you most of all to the animals in my life—Lola, Nemo, Dory, Porchie, and New Cat—for continuously teaching me the importance of honoring the value and autonomy of another living being's life. The perspective you've given me on the world and our relationship with animals is what shaped the reason for writing this book. I wanted to pass on what you have taught me: that so much is possible with understanding, curiosity, and love.

Did you enjoy this book?

WRITE A REVIEW!

REVIEWS HELP OTHER READERS DECIDE ON THEIR NEXT
BOOK! GO TO WWW.DOGWISE.COM AND SELECT A STAR
RATING (1-5) THEN LEAVE SOME COMMENTS DESCRIBING
WHAT YOU ENJOYED OR SOMETHING YOU LEARNED WHILE
READING THIS BOOK!

Dogwise™
All things dog.

Connect with us

FOLLOW, LIKE, AND TAG US ON SOCIAL
MEDIA TO STAY CONNECTED

SCAN THE QR CODES BELOW WITH YOUR PHONE'S CAMERA
APP TO GO DIRECTLY TO OUR SOCIAL MEDIA PROFILES

instagram
@dogwise.books

facebook
/dogwise

twitter
@DogwiseBooks

Made in United States
North Haven, CT
06 August 2024

55754470R00109